Healing and Recovering from Pornography

Fighting Addictions, Viewed from a Biblical Perspective

By Ivan Chamurliev

Copyright © 2024 Ivan Chamurliev

All rights reserved. This book or any portion thereof may not be reproduced or used in any manner whatsoever without the express written permission of the publisher except for the use of brief quotations in a book review.

All Scripture quotations are taken from the New King James Version of the Bible. Copyright © 1982 by Thomas Nelson, Inc. Used by permission. All rights reserved.

Visit the author's website at
bible-meditations.my.canva.site
or contact him at
ivan.chamurliev@gmail.com

Table of Contents

Introduction

What I wrote in this book is a very sensitive topic, and we need to examine all and be cautious when it comes to this issue, as this is about our lives.

This book contains some very practical and simple advice on how to quit the issue of porn addiction and walk that road despite having difficulties. These guidelines could be applied to any other addiction, as addictions affect us pretty much in the same way, even though they are different, and there are common practices we can apply to fight all of them.

Although the subtitle of this book suggests that it is mainly for believers, and the issue of porn addiction is seen from a Christian perspective, you can get some practical advice in this book on how to quit a porn addiction or other kinds of addictions, even though you do not share the same opinion regarding life and you do not believe. Each person is free to decide for himself. One does not believe in Christ only for the issues he might be having with addictions, but still, a person faces challenges better when he believes.

What could help us if we see it from a Christian perspective is that Christians base their lives on the Bible and their faith in God, who clearly rejects addiction and is not pleased with it. He commands us to live a clean life. Even without being believers and followers of Christ, we can see that the issue of addiction brings consequences and other problems in our lives.

Why is this happening? Because we are not meant to live in such a way. This is one of the reasons why God, who knows us more than anyone else, prohibited these things. When God tells us in His Word not to live in sin, it is because He knows this is not good for us. It could hurt us physically or emotionally.

This is the point by which you can see that this is not good and how what you find in this book can help you. You can choose a side, see it as a believer or a non-believer, and get some practical advice. Still, the main purpose is to get free and live a plentiful, victorious life.

Chapter 1

The Truth about Porn

How can we avoid addictions such as porn? Do we realize what it is about, and what is God's opinion toward it? Do believers struggle with it?

In today's days, more than ever, this kind of issue is common and becoming more normal by the day. Some people don't even acknowledge it as a problem until it starts to bring severe consequences in someone's life. We need to notice that porn usage has increased drastically in these recent times, as the internet is now available to everyone—as are portable smart devices. It is much easier than ever to obtain it.

Before this technology was widely available, you probably had to hide (if you were underage), sneak to the newsstand, or even send someone to get it for you. Now, times are different. People say that we develop, and the advancement of technology helps us have a better life. I am not against technology, as because of it I am able to write to you now. Still, what is the actual price we need to pay for having all of this comfort and easy lifestyle the technology provides us? It's high, in any case.

According to some statistics, in America alone, 200,000 adults are considered porn addicts among the country's 40 million porn consumers. Just imagine how many there are worldwide.

37 videos are made every day in the United States alone.

28,000 people are watching it every given moment.

Recent statistics show that today, roughly 2.5 million people visit the world's most popular porn sites every 60 seconds.

About $3,000 is spent every second on pornographic material.

Just the hardcore pornography titles released in the US in 1988 were around 1,300, while in 2005, they were increased to 13,588. Just imagine how many there are today.

These are some common statistics you can find anywhere, and they might not be so accurate, as they keep increasing. Still, we are not here to talk about statistics but rather about what this topic means and how it can affect our lives. How can we protect ourselves from it?

Obviously, statistics are needed to show how humans degraded for such a short time having this kind of technology available and the ability to use it. Where are we headed if we reach this point in such a short period of time? Obviously, someone might say, "But there is nothing so wrong with watching porn." Yes, according to someone, but we, being Christians know God doesn't approve of it. Matthew 5:27–28 says:

> "You have heard that it was said to those of old, 'You shall not commit adultery.' But I say to you that whoever looks at a woman to lust for her has already committed adultery with her in his heart."

These verses state that just looking at a woman with lust is adultery in the heart. God has established that a man and a woman should have a proper relationship when they are together. He invented sex, but people just misused it. It is so because we live in a sinful society, but this nevertheless cannot be an excuse.

If we know what is right, we must strive to do it. God forbids certain things and sins because He knows they can harm us. He created us, and He knows best what is good for us and what can damage us. We don't, instead. This is the reason He forbids sin. Why is it that He forbids lying, for example? Because He is complete truth, and there is no deceit in Him. The other reason is also that He knows that lying can hurt the other person, and this can push him to seek revenge. In this way, things can get more complicated.

Why is it that He forbids the offense toward another person? For the same reason. A person gets hurt because of that, and a simple verbal offense could grow into something bigger. The same is true with all the rest of the sins, including the sins having to do with lust. He forbids them because He is holy, and His nature cannot bear any sin and iniquity, but also because all of these things can hurt us and grow into something bigger. They are not good for us.

He is our Creator, and He knows best what is good for us and what is not. We have been designed to function in a specific way, and each deviation can hurt us emotionally and even physically in some cases. There are *consequences* for each sin.

So, going back to the topic of porn, we Christians mustn't have it as a practice, first because God is not pleased with it because it is a sin, and second because of its consequences. The second reason is something many people have gone through, even not being believers and godly people. They know there are consequences because they have experienced them. These are consequences that can tear families apart and reduce someone's ability to have a normal life. There are many therapeutic groups with the purpose of quitting porn that are not faith-based, and the persons leading them are not believers.

Ordinary people know there are consequences of the wrong style of life because they have experienced them. Still, they don't know the main reason for which we mustn't do those things. The reason is that the wrong style of life is sinful, and God is not pleased with sin. It hurts Him, and it hurts us, as we are created according to His image. We are not created and meant to live in such a way. We, as Christians, have a double reason to avoid it in our lives and resist it because we know the Father's heart.

As it happens in any addiction, we can't see the destructive outcome immediately, but when it comes, it might be too late. Nevertheless, I am here to tell you there is a solution, and there is *hope*. It is not me telling you this, but the Bible. There are always consequences anyway, but a person can be healed.

A lot of families and relationships suffer due to porn usage. One study observed that men who started watching porn increased their risk of divorce from 5% to 10%; for women, it was from 6% to 18%. 56% of divorce cases involve one party having an obsessive interest in pornographic websites.

No one should feel invincible when it comes to this topic, thinking it will never happen to him. We are all vulnerable to it. We are created in such a way. We naturally have sexual desires, and we need to satisfy them. Still, it needs to be done in the right way. We naturally have it, and the enemy knows about it. Some people think that being married or having a relationship will help them resist and not give in to a porn addiction, but statistics say that married persons are also vulnerable to it. I write this as a non-married single person, and therefore, I know the difficulties this condition brings. Still, there is a way to resist it and have victory.

According to scientists, there is an area in your brain known as the "reward center" that helps form habits. One of the chemicals that this area releases is called "dopamine." When this chemical is released, you feel pleasure, satisfaction, and motivation. When you feel good after achieving something, it is because you have a surge of dopamine in your brain. Let's say that dopamine is like the reward we receive after an effort we make. After achieving something, your brain releases it.

This is also what helps us to be motivated. It could be the motivation to build something, to create something, or simply to provide for our livelihood. Having sex is also something that triggers the release of dopamine. God made it in a way for us to feel the pleasure of it and to stimulate procreation in a natural way. The pleasure we feel after making efforts and achieving something we aim for is like our reward. This is what helps us to develop as well. This is what helps us to be stimulated to perform specific work or anything else there might be.

God also rewards His people when they believe in Him, depend on Him, and follow His will. He created the pleasure of receiving an award after heavy work. This happens with the purpose that we can perform certain actions to pursue that reward. Being with a member of the opposite sex and having a relationship is also a kind of reward—something that we aim to because we are naturally made in this way.

The problem is when we achieve dopamine release in a non-natural way. Drugs can trigger the release of dopamine. Any addiction does. When you, for example, work hard the whole month and get paid, you feel good about it, as you know that with the salary received, you can provide everything needed for yourself. This is what also stimulates you to work.

When instead of working hard, you play a lottery and instantly win that same amount of money or more, you feel good at that moment because, without much effort, you get to the same state of satisfaction as when you worked hard. That is the moment of reward. It is the moment of satisfaction. Your brain knows it and instantly releases a huge amount of chemicals, causing you to feel pleasure because of it.

What is wrong is that this wasn't natural but artificially produced. In the very beginning, this kind of satisfaction was placed there so that we could serve God and enjoy a relationship with Him. He is not like a tyrant who makes us serve Him without the pleasure of doing that. What happened next is that man fell into sin and all we had as feelings and emotions got messed up as the most important was missing, which was God.

It happens that when you receive pleasure from drugs or pornography (anything that triggers the pleasure in a non-natural way), you receive this pleasure without putting much effort into it. It is not like a reward anymore, but something that is due to you and that you selfishly consume and look for. The devil offers sex without love. He diminishes us as people looking merely for our primal feelings and senses without what is most important and what stands behind them.

God invented love in general and specifically the love between man and woman. In the times in which we live, the word "love" is being used much less, and feelings and relationships have become plastic and artificial, reduced just to the consumption of it and not to something more profound. People in our culture today even prefer not to marry. Their relationship is based mainly on interests.

Meanwhile, the Bible tells us in 1 Corinthians 13:5 that love "does not seek its own." Some partners may even consent to the other one to have other relationships as long as this doesn't affect their benefits. Watching porn, for example, is like going straight to the senses and the pleasure we feel from sex but without going through everything that comes before that. A man is supposed to gain the trust of a woman. He is supposed to win her heart, and then receive the reward.

With prostitution and porn, this process is totally neglected, and what God meant by all of this is being perverted and reduced to the feeling itself. A feeling with which we are created with a purpose to complete the whole picture of how God sees love and relationship so that we can live in a proper way. We have to live out the entire meaning of what a relationship between a man and a woman should be, not just a part of it based on instinct. An instinct that is rightly placed in us, but taking it out and focusing just on it can set us off track and live in the wrong way with the wrong consequences.

The devil is using all of this and making out of it a weak spot through which he can attack us. We are created with all these feelings and senses, with the ability to feel passion, joy, anger, and pleasure. The problem is not in these feelings alone but in the fact that we lack God in our lives. He is the missing piece in our lives. He is the piece of the puzzle through which we are complete. Without Him, we are guided by our passions and desires, but we need to be guided by Him instead.

So, the problem is not that we have these feelings and passions but that we miss Him in our lives. Without Him, all these things that we are created with become a sin instead of a blessing for us. Like porn, drugs and other addictions trigger pleasure in us. They go straight away for it. We are created to enjoy these kinds of feelings, and that's why we get addicted to them. They are created in us so that we can have a time in which we can rest and not feel over-exhausted and tired.

God made them for our good. Instead, we often misuse them. Pleasure is there so a man can receive it after heavy laboring and fatigue. It needs to come after an effort after we achieve something. That's why dopamine is released after we finish a job well done, for example.

The fast-achieved pleasure is received in a non-natural way because we haven't labored for it. I know it may sound harsh, but when experiencing this kind of pleasure achieved in a synthetic way (including pornography), we become like parasites.

Here are some articles that provide us with facts about the topic.

"Dopamine is known as a "pleasure" chemical; it creates a link between certain habits and a "reward." Activities like exercise, eating, and sex all trigger reactions in this part of the brain.

With pornography, however, the brain responds differently than it does with run-of-the-mill stimulation, like a sugary snack or a simple game. For most daily behaviors, the brain has an "off" switch that stops the release of dopamine once a craving has been satisfied.

In contrast, pornography impacts the brain much like an addictive drug by triggering ever-increasing amounts of dopamine. Over time, the brain builds up a tolerance to the excess dopamine and requires either more access or more extreme content (or sometimes both) to achieve that same level of perceived pleasure.

Research from a *Neuroscience of Internet Pornography Addiction* report indicates that extended exposure to pornography correlates with less activity in the brain's reward circuit.

Furthermore, once the reward center is altered by "free" dopamine triggers like porn, it can lead to a person compulsively seeking out the activity that triggered the dopamine discharge." [1]

"Many abused substances directly trigger dopamine secretion–without us having to work to accomplish a goal. This can damage the dopamine reward system. In porn, we get "sex" without the work of courtship. Now, scans show that porn can alter the reward center too." [2]

"Drugs such as cocaine can cause a big, fast increase of dopamine in your brain. That satisfies your natural reward system in a big way. But repeated drug use also raises the threshold for this kind of pleasure. This means you need to take more to get the same high. Meanwhile, drugs make your body less able to produce dopamine naturally. This leads to emotional lows when you're sober." [3]

As we said before, if we feel pleasure today, it is because God allows it; I mean that it is because He invented it. There is a passage in Ecclesiastes that describes it well.

¹⁸ Here is what I have seen: *It is* good and fitting *for one* to eat and drink, and to enjoy the good of all his labor in which he toils under the sun all the days of his life which God gives him; for it *is* his heritage. ¹⁹ As for every man to whom God has given riches and wealth, and given him power to eat of it, to receive his heritage and rejoice in his labor—this *is* the gift of God. (Ecclesiastes 5:18–19)

This passage explains that for a man to rejoice and feel pleasure is possible because God allows him that. He has placed these feelings in him. As we said before, the problem is that man has misused this gift, and this is for the only reason that he lacks God in his life. Not knowing God and not having Him in his life leaves a man to deal with all these feelings and passions he has, alone and without a guide.

When God fills somebody's life, that person doesn't feel the rush to fill himself with something else or abuse it. He will do everything with a measure and will be content with the state he is in, as it is said in 1 Timothy 6:6:

"Now godliness with contentment is great gain."

He gives us the living water with which we are really satisfied. A man of God still feels pleasures and will look for them but without exaggerating and without doing them in a wrong way. Sex, for example, is not a sin in itself if done with one's own spouse; but when done in another way, it is wrong.

A man of God will not only do those things in the right way, but will also have as a goal to be patient and wait for the right time when these things will be done in the right way. He is already satisfied because God is in his life, which greatly helps him fight the wrong passions. I am not speaking about religion here, but about truly knowing Jesus and having Him in your heart. This is what really helps.

That's why when we talk about pornography in this book, and we speak about people struggling with it and about believers struggling, we need to say that having a relationship with God and knowing Him is truly something essential, as we are not only speaking about some practical advice, even if they are also found in this book. The most important and essential part is Jesus and the strength He can give us. This is why, while we are in temptation, we need to pray and trust in God to help us and give us strength.

Some things are stronger than our own ability or morality, or things we do to avoid falling into sin. Here, we are talking of very basic fleshly desires we have. Sexual desires are not comparable to any other sin or temptation. We cannot compare them with stealing or lying, for example. When someone wants to steal something, he plans it and deliberately falls into it. In most cases, that person might not be a believer.

Instead, when we speak about a sexual desire, it can happen at the moment when someone least expects it. This is because this is part of our nature and desires. What happens is that it needs to be done in the right way with the right person.

But what happens is that while we wait for that, we still have these passions in us. They are not taken away from us and returned afterward when we need them. We keep on having them. Still, we want to please God, and we abstain from them. That's why believers are more vulnerable to falling into those things rather than falling into something else. Because these are the major sins that still live in their members, as Romans 7:23 tells us:

> "But I see another law in my members,
> warring against the law of my mind, and
> bringing me into captivity to the law of
> sin which is in *my members*." (Romans
> 7:23, emphasis added)

All the rest of the sins are something that most believers can decide to do or not, and as they fear God, they will do everything possible to avoid them. But when discussing sexual desires, we talk about something living in our members. It is placed there, and it is an instinct not wrong by itself, but it could be done in the wrong way. We are speaking about fleshly desires here.

This is one of the things that I think Paul was describing when talking in Romans 7 about what he wanted to do well but it was happening the opposite in the end.

> "For what I am doing, I do not
> understand. For what I will to do, that I
> do not practice; but what I hate, that I
> do." (Romans 7:15)

This is what can occur in the life of a Christian, and of course that he was talking about sin in general—any sin might be there, but we can apply this scripture for sins related to sex. We are not only talking about adultery but also about any sin related to sexual desire. A person of faith, however, can fall into adultery, but the consequences are painful.

We have the example of King David, and we see the huge consequences he brought in his life by falling into it (2 Samuel 11). I am not saying that this is something that will necessarily always prevail over the believer. God is exhorting us through His word to resist and fight sin. This shows us that He will also give us the means to do it. Chapter 7 of Romans finishes with the verses saying:

> "O wretched man that I am! Who will
> deliver me from this body of death? I

thank God—through Jesus Christ our Lord!

So then, with the mind I myself serve the law of God, but with the flesh the law of sin." (Romans 7:24–25, emphasis added)

This passage indicates that there is a solution as after mourning about the weakness of his flesh and asking who will deliver him from the body of death, the apostle Paul thanks God.

We can talk about pornography, which is something so diffused in today's society, or even about masturbation, which also falls under this group of sins. I know that some people condemn it, and others accept it as something normal. *The solution*, though, when we struggle with a sin or when we sinned is not in reducing the guilt by excusing ourselves or taking the act of sin (I am talking about any sin) as something normal, but by *going to Jesus and having faith*.

It is also not a question of just condemning it (masturbation) but understanding the reason for which it happens, understanding the root of the problem, and resisting it in a genuine way. We need to know that by itself, it is not right.

I know that when talking about sin, we cannot divide it into less and more sinful because sinning in itself is not right in God's eyes. Still, we can say that not all sins are on the same level, even though we see that one could lead to the other. We need, though, to fight sin while in its conception.

> "But each one is tempted when he is
> drawn away by his own desires and
> enticed. Then, when desire has
> conceived, it gives birth to sin; and sin,
> when it is full-grown, brings forth death."
> (James 1:14–15)

This passage talks of how sin grows, beginning from a desire. That is the point where we need to focus and fight. If we also don't have the right opinion about sin and the realization of how sinful it is, then we can say we lost a huge part of the battle from the very beginning.

When we get to the final stage of sin—the one expressed in a greater sinful act with huge consequences—we will become aware that we did wrong and sinned, and we will be very displeased, but this attitude toward sin must be there from the beginning.

Suppose for someone it is not wrong to tease himself with certain images, even though they are not as explicit as some others, or to enter into certain conversations or to flirt with any woman. In that case, it is no wonder that he can soon fall into the trap of sin and when that happens, he will certainly be displeased.

Sometimes, it is too late to fix situations and wounds we caused to others or avoid some consequences. Of course, God can still forgive us if we have faith, but here we are speaking about avoiding sin so that we can avoid the consequences, as they are painful.

Do you remember what happened to David or Samson? David lost his son from Bathsheba, which he had from the adultery committed with her, and nearly lost his kingdom by the hand of his own son Absalom (2 Samuel 12:14–3, 2 Samuel 15–18).

Samson was blinded after revealing the secret of his strength to Delilah and then died together with the Philistines when asking God to give him strength for the last time so that he could fight his enemies for the last time.

Could those people have lived in a different way by being more cautious with sin? We cannot exactly answer this question, as we are humans just like them, but I think a person could avoid certain tough situations in his life by avoiding sin. Yes, of course, we all sin—and we will sin—but we could avoid making the situation worse with sin. We will all have wrong desires, but we mustn't let them grow into something bigger.

I'm not promoting human perfection with what I am saying and with what I am about to tell, as we know that the most important for someone and what really makes him holy and clean in front of God is the blood of Christ. I am also not trying to compare sins and make it look like if someone didn't commit certain sins as another person, he is better and holier than him.

If that person, even though not having committed the same sins as someone else, is not cleansed by the blood of the lamb, then he is not better than any other person. And the opposite, if the other person has committed sins but repented after that, he really is clean. Jesus also tells us not to sin anymore, but the point here is to be washed by the blood of Christ.

I am talking against sin and sinning because of the consequences it brings and because it hurts us. It is painful for us because we haven't been created to live in such a way, and God knows what is best for us. Sin also hurts His heart, of course. It hurts His heart, and it harms us.

If we compare them, we can place sexual sins in this order: lust, masturbation, pornography, and adultery. The worst we can say is adultery, but we cannot say that by not committing it, we are right. We need to fight with all of them.

We can say that masturbation is not on the same level as watching pornography, but falling continuously in it and not resisting it at all can lead to the next stage. Why? Because practicing it as something regular will stop satisfying us, and we will eventually want more, and we may sin in a worse way.

It all starts, though, with lust, and this is the point from which we need to take on it and fight it. Jesus rightly pointed out that adultery is committed in the heart (Matthew 5:27–28). This is because He can give us strength to overcome it. In ancient days, people referred to adultery just as a physically committed act, while Jesus pointed out that it starts from the heart and condemned it as a sin.

He didn't do that to condemn us, saying there is no solution, as all of us sinned this way. He said it to help us be really clean and prevent us from sinning in a worse way. He also provides a way to help and give us a solution through His Spirit. This is also why He died for us—to forgive our sins but also to help us fight and resist sin by giving us His power and Spirit.

When a person fights sin from the starting point—his heart—and overcomes it, he is really clean. This is something we cannot achieve with our strength. Faith is needed. Still, when we start fighting it from the heart, we can prevent many other sinful actions that could come after it.

I also repeat that the main solution to all is being satisfied with Jesus and having Him in our lives. This is what will really help us prevent sinning. Obviously, we are made of flesh, and neglecting some of the sins in their embryonic stage, and falling into them repeatedly, leads us to more.

Placing pornography before adultery on our list and not making it look as bad as it mustn't comfort us or let us think that as long as we do that occasionally and don't commit adultery, we are fine. As we said already, sin is usually escalating, and if we do it freely without trying to stop or prevent it, it is much more likely to grow into something else.

> "Then, when desire has conceived, it gives birth to sin; and sin, when it is full-grown, brings forth death." (James 1:15)

Anything causing us to sin is wrong, but what is worse with pornography is that it can easily become an idol and addiction. When we have an addiction or we give priority to something, it steals our time. We can't focus in a proper way on what is really important; we can't focus on God. I was addicted to substances in my past life before knowing Jesus, and I know how it feels. When you are addicted to something, you depend on it.

Still, I depended on other things, too, after my conversion. I am not necessarily speaking of obviously sinful things in this case, but of something that is apparently normal. With time, I noticed that I was kind of addicted to it and had it as an idol.

Idolizing something and addiction go hand in hand. We can say they are the same. These are things we love, and they steal our time. They take the place of God in our life. We still say that we love Him, but He is not in the first place in our hearts. I am not saying we cannot do things we love, but all needs to be done in order—giving priority to God.

He deserves the first place, and He knows that If He is not there, we can quickly be overwhelmed by other things and forget our faith. That's why He is a jealous God.

To have an idol is a sin. We can talk about idols as things that are apparently not sinful by themselves, but we need to be careful because we can abuse them. We can take as examples common things such as watching our favorite TV show, sports, clothing, food, and exercising.

These things are not sinful by themselves but can turn into idols, stealing our energy and time. We need to learn to make use of them in the right way.

How can we recognize that something has turned into an idol for us? When it takes the time that we usually dedicate to something else which is also important to us, especially when it steals the time we need to dedicate to the Lord—when we are obsessed with those things and we spend most of the day thinking about them. Paul said in 1 Corinthians 6:12:

> "All things are lawful for me, but all
> things are not helpful. All things are
> lawful for me, but I will not be brought
> under the power of any."

Here he referred to something not sinful by itself, but he said that we could be brought under its power, and in this way, it could become an idol in our lives. The Lord opposes idol worship in the Bible and places it amongst the things He is mostly not pleased with.

Many of the kings in the Old Testament lost their blessings from God, and He wasn't pleased with them due to idol worship. At that time, there were wooden or gold idols related to certain practices, but in our times could be the things we are doing or using in our everyday lives.

We still can make use of those things. as they are not sinful, but if we see that they control us, we need to be careful and reduce or totally cut their usage in some cases. This is a topic that has to do also with the matter we mentioned before, that certain things might be sinful for some people or might induce them to sin, while for others might not have the same effect. That's why we always need to examine ourselves and be really sincere about our condition.

When talking about porn, we are obviously talking about something that is sinful by itself. Our heart, anyway, is easily seduced to go after any kind of idol and could turn anything into an idol. About porn, we can say that it can be turned into an idol more easily than anything else because we have the natural desire to be with the opposite sex, as it is given to us so that we can enjoy a relationship.

God thought even of that. He wanted to reward us and make us feel pleasure. What happened is that man had abused this gift. When watching porn, it is as if we are taken to the situation to see with our eyes a sexual act; in this way, our eyes send a signal to our brain, which produces dopamine on his side. We naturally have an attraction toward it, and that's why we become easily addicted and have it as an idol.

If we know that we can quickly feel this kind of pleasure by just clicking a link, we will be tempted to do it. Some people say that we need to follow our instincts and nature, but this is not the way it needs to be done.

We cannot follow this path, as all our feelings are often messed up due to what is missing in us. This is God and the self-control He can provide. With Him, we cannot use and follow our instincts and feelings properly.

Worshipping idols was one of the main sins the Israeli nation committed in the Old Testament times. This is also the sin that makes God upset and hurts Him the most. It is because He had commanded us to love Him above everything (Deuteronomy 10:12).

To idolize porn is more seductive than anything else because, as we said before, it is in us to have sexual desires. We are created with them, but we are meant to use them in a proper way. This is one of the sins that entices us more easily than all the other sins.

We are easily introduced to fall into addictions and idolatry, as these two are the same thing. We naturally have the ability to live and desire something, to be passionate about something. The problem is just that without God, we are following the wrong things—and even if we seek to do something right, we follow it and love it in the wrong way.

Because it is God who helps us and makes us complete. With Him, we function properly and in the right way. With Him, we can properly love our neighbor and our family and attend properly to life and its matters. Not knowing Jesus and having a proper relationship with Him will make us see Christianity as just an abstention from all. It is not in this way because God allows us the pleasures, but done in the right way. This, and having Jesus in our hearts (which is the most important), will help us have a fully satisfied and happy life.

Happiness is not something that many people can achieve. Most think it consists of having everything in abundance and allowing themselves to do anything they want. Even so, they realize they still don't feel happy and see happiness as something not achievable.

It is not in this way with believers. They are satisfied, even when they have less. That's why Paul said in Philippians 4:12 that he has learned to live in each situation he was in—in scarcity and abundance. This is only possible because of the gospel. This is not just an ideology that helps us know that we will have a reward one day (which is true), but because Jesus can really satisfy our life now, in this life.

A believer is happy in any situation because of God's strength in his life. With this, I am not saying that believers don't have complaints at all or that they don't feel down, and their heart doesn't go after what their eyes see sometimes. I am saying that, generally speaking, they are fine, and their major concern and desire is to follow God because they know He is the good shepherd who leads them in green pastures and satisfies their soul.

The other thing we can say about porn is that it reduces men and women just to primitive creatures instead of being humans with dignity. The way especially women are treated is humiliating. If a young individual who is growing and learning gets to explore and learn about love and sex and has porn as an educational and teaching method, then he is already growing up with the completely wrong idea of what sex is. I am not saying there mustn't be any pleasure or fun in a sexual act, but if we take the porn industry as a main example, then we are indeed wrong. We can see how, with time, the exhibitions, videos, and scenes in adult movies have become more violent and depraved. This is because of the state of man, which is also deteriorating.

Chapter 2

Practical Advice

How can we avoid porn addiction? We said that common persons are affected and tempted by it, and we said that believers are also tempted. This chapter sheds a bit more light on this question, and I will also try to give you some practical advice on the matter. We already said that the main way is to pray, trust in God, and be a believer. Being a believer, even if this is something fundamental, is not all when we talk about wrestling with our flesh and avoiding such a temptation.

I am saying this because the Bible says there might be different types of Christians; I mean that some of them might be building on their foundation with gold, silver, precious stones, and other materials, which endure more efficiently to fire and temptations. Others build with wood, hay, or straw, which are materials that tend to perish. And, the scriptures say that those persons will suffer loss but will be saved, yet so as through fire, meaning that they will suffer in this life due to the cause of sin.

The foundation is Christ, and the materials we use to build are the way we live and dedicate our lives to Him. Building our lives on Christ as a foundation is a huge step and success, but then we need to live life in a proper way as He has commanded us so that we can obtain victory.

> ¹² Now if anyone builds on this foundation *with* gold, silver, precious stones, wood, hay, straw, ¹³ each one's work will become clear; for the Day will declare it, because it will be revealed by fire; and the fire will test each one's work, of what sort it is. ¹⁴ If anyone's work which he has built on *it* endures, he will receive a reward. ¹⁵ If anyone's work is burned, he will suffer loss; but he himself will be saved, yet so as through fire. (1 Corinthians 3:12–15)

Many Christians have suffered, but some did for more noble causes such as persecution for the gospel. The Bible tells us that if we suffer, it mustn't be for something wrong we have done but for Christ's sake (1 Peter 4:15–16).

We are also exhorted to be watchful. If we are exhorted to watch, which means that we could be sleeping as well. My opinion is that if someone plays with fire, then not only his works but also he can burn himself. This is a personal opinion, though.

One thing for sure is that when we only suffer for the cause of sin, God works in our lives, but we don't grow as much as when we suffer for the right cause. We remain small in faith. The purpose is that we can bring fruit to others. We could miss this when we are only focused on fighting our own battles because we keep falling.

I will not be too harsh on this argument, though, as I have also been on one and the other side. I am writing to counsel and help those who struggle with this issue. We have to rise if we fall by finding forgiveness and looking for ways to improve by strengthening ourselves through faith. He wants to raise us up.

Finding the root of our problem

So, if we want to be Christians who build with proper materials like precious stones and gold (figuratively speaking), we need to be diligent and seek God's guidance, wisdom, and strength above all so that we can avoid temptation. It is Him who helps us with the temptations in the first place.

> "And do not lead us into temptation,
> But deliver us from the evil one.
> For Yours is the kingdom and the power
> and the glory forever. Amen." (Matthew
> 6:13)

Then, of course, our part is understanding what is good for our life and what is wrong. We all know that the root of our temptation and problem is sin. Still, sometimes, there are things that are not necessarily obviously sinful but can lead us to be tempted. They are like an igniting button. These are the things we need to discover. For example, if I know that watching certain TV shows or commercials with ads that show some explicit content could trigger something in me so that I can fall afterward into something worse, I will avoid watching it. Even if that content in itself is not apparently sinful, it could trigger a desire and lead me to it.

Some other people, for example, might not be so vulnerable toward that particular content, but I need to look at myself first. If I know myself and my weaknesses, I must avoid certain situations. Obviously, there will be times and situations where some things cannot be avoided under certain circumstances.

Still, in another situation, when I could do something to avoid what is wrong, it is my responsibility. Speaking about each person's weaknesses and their differences, we can see a passage in which Paul explains that:

> "All things are lawful for me, but not all
> things are helpful; all things are lawful
> for me, but not all things edify."
> (1 Corinthians 10:23)

This passage refers to persons with weaknesses in the faith and talks about certain things that might harm their conscience. All of us can include ourselves in this number because we are all weak in something. It is not because those particular things are sinful but because they might remind us of sin and lead us to something else.

The passage mentioned above is similar to the one we mentioned before in 1 Corinthians 6:12. The passages coming after it mention sexual immorality.

> [12] All things are lawful for me, but all
> things are not helpful. All things are
> lawful for me, but I will not be brought
> under the power of any. [13] Foods for the
> stomach and the stomach for foods, but
> God will destroy both it and them. Now
> the body *is* not for sexual immorality
> but for the Lord, and the Lord for the
> body. [14] And God both raised up the
> Lord and will also raise us up by His
> power. (1 Corinthians 6:12–14)

It is not shameful for a person to acknowledge his weaknesses. On the contrary, God helps those who see themselves as weak and recognize their weaknesses rather than those who think they are strong enough to make it by themselves.

Each person is vulnerable in a certain area. If watching certain things, being someplace, or doing something that could lead us to or trigger sinful desires, then we need to avoid it. To somebody else, it might be different. He might be weak in another area.

That's why Paul said that all things are lawful (permissible) for him, but he won't be brought under the power of any (1 Corinthians 6:12). He wanted to say that some people are weak for certain things and those things can become a problem for them and control them.

Talking about avoiding sin, we need to say something fundamental about it, and this is that according to the measure someone understands grace or gives value to godly things, salvation, grace, and God; in that way, he will also try to avoid sin and avoid displeasing God. He knows the value of it.

He might not always succeed for the reason that He might have neglected some fundamental things such as watching, praying, and seeking God's wisdom. He could become weaker in the Spirit in this way, but he would know the value of what God gave him and would eventually fight with sin and temptations. He will try not to repeat that sin. That will be his desire.

If it happens, it will be for negligence, and he will bear the consequences. The way someone fell into sin and how he repented is also very important. If he knows the value of salvation and grace (at least in part as all our life we would have to learn), he will also be displeased for the sin and go brokenhearted to God, asking for forgiveness and restoration.

The one who doesn't feel remorse at all in front of God (not only in front of people) probably doesn't know God and has never accepted Jesus in his heart. Salvation and grace help you understand the value of godly things and God Himself, as He is the one who gifted you that. After receiving them, you feel eternally grateful.

Some ways to avoid falling into the trap

Another practical piece of advice I can give is what I've done after realizing that I am vulnerable to falling into the temptation of pornography. I tried to avoid certain apps on my phone and even deleted some after a while. I repeat that here, we are not discussing something obviously sinful but something that may trigger a desire in us and lead us to sin.

If, on some social media applications, you may see some medium-level explicit content that you know triggers something in you, then you need to avoid it. If not, you can at least set the app preferences to avoid explicit content. If you see that this is not enough and you still see something, then you need to use it more rarely or even delete it.

I'll tell you why deleting it is a better option sometimes. This app (I am just giving an example here with an app; it might be anything else) will stay on your phone because you left it on your phone, as you considered it something not apparently dangerous. Sometimes, you might feel something calling you to open it just for a bit. You are not doing this with the purpose of sinning, as you are a believer. Something is just calling you to open that app, and you might do it as apparently for you it is not dangerous.

Sometimes, I even said to myself, "Maybe this, after all, is not that dangerous; let me see if it really is so that I can know what to do." *This is the reason you have in your mind while your subconscious knows that you might see something there, and subconsciously, you want to do it for that reason.*

I can reckon that by feeling my heart beating heavily before taking such actions. This is because I know what I could find there. This is the way believers could be tempted and fall into sin. Ordinary people who don't know God, and most probably don't even fight temptation, as they don't find a reason to resist it, don't feel that way.

Many of them deliberately fall into sin. Still, the devil uses different tactics when tempting a child of God. When we are not spiritually strong, because we haven't fed ourselves with the Word of God and we are not being watchful, the enemy uses this kind of tactic to let us fall, and he might succeed if we are not aware of that.

I am explaining to you how our subconscious might work to tempt us, but to know this and to be aware only is not the main solution. What we need to do, first of all, is to be close to God and to be spiritually prepared.

That's why the Bible states that the heart is the most deceitful of all things (Jeremiah 17:9). Our own heart deceives us, and its intentions are like a deep well; we cannot know them straight away. The same example could be applied to any other situation or addiction. For example, when coming back from work, we almost subconsciously pass by the way we know we shouldn't, as there we might find what we need to stay away from.

There are things much more important than social media or other things you like: your spiritual health. We need to be sincere with ourselves regarding this matter and understand our weaknesses without hiding them. This is for our good.

When we see that something is not good for us and we are in a time in which we know we are more vulnerable, we need to cut off doing certain things that might lead us to something wrong, at least for some time.

It is not a question of cutting everything in all the cases, but just what we see as more threatening. I never quit using my electronic devices, but just some things that I perceived as threatening, such as some applications, visiting specific sites, etc.

I repeat that here, I am not talking about something obviously sinful. The sites and the applications I quit using didn't contain any explicit material, but they could trigger something in me and awaken a sinful desire.

This is what I personally did for the matter; then, each person needs to examine himself and be extremely sincere with himself about this. Do you need to quit using your electronic devices for some time? Then you need to do it.

I didn't do it then because I was in the middle of writing a book and needed to finish it. Still, you need to examine the reason why you need to use your devices and see if it is really necessary for you to keep using them.

You can leave them for a certain time or reduce the time you use them. We need to know that after falling into porn, there is a time in which you are more vulnerable to it. There are programs and applications you can use to block adult content on your PC and phone. You might ask a friend of yours or someone you trust to monitor you by installing that application, too. These are the ones that parents use to monitor their kids, and even though you are not a kid, you need to look for any way or help that can prevent you from stumbling.

Apps and adult blocker programs could be useful because they could block content before it reaches you. Believe me, even though we are strong, it is easy to be drawn into those kinds of temptations when we are in front of them.

When a drug addict or alcoholic gets through a time without consuming, they might not always be tempted when in front of a temptation of that kind because their body and mind have already healed in a way—and they won't feel the same rush as when they would feel it in the first couple of months for example. It is not the same when talking about sexual desires and addictions. We might get better with time, but we will always feel that rush when in front of them. It is different compared to other addictions. That's why we need to find a way to be exposed as few times as possible to what can trigger those desires in us. The Bible gives us direct and practical advice regarding the matter in Proverbs 6:27–28.

> "Can a man take fire to his bosom,
> And his clothes not be burned?
> Can one walk on hot coals,
> And his feet not be seared?"

This passage follows other passages about being aware of an evil woman and seductress. It means that sometimes we mustn't play with temptation, even if it is small. That's why, when possible, we need to avoid all situations and things that could trigger our wrong desires. Coal by itself is something small, and at times, it doesn't look like it could start a fire, but it does.

Using certain apps and programs to block them, as we mentioned before, or even asking someone to assist us is not a bad idea. Before the technological advancement we witnessed in the past decades, it was harder to get to that material. Often, while looking for a way to provide it, you could've as well changed your mind and repented from your desire.

Today, these things are just there for you with a single click, and sometimes they impose themselves without asking. That's why we need to acknowledge our weak points and do what is possible with the help of God and the help of other believers, too.

We must be open about our issues and problems in the church or with brothers in faith who we feel are close to us. This is also the reason to commune with other believers. Not only to discuss biblical passages, which is right, but also to confess our weaknesses to each other, pray for each other, and sustain each other.

This is what the Bible tells us to do. This, together with acknowledging our weak points and having faith in

God, is one of the main keys. Sometimes, we state that we are all sinners, and each one falls short in something, but we don't specify our sins or deal with them. This is not right, and the Bible doesn't teach us this way.

We do all this because we want to prioritize our spiritual condition, and a spiritual person will always prioritize his spiritual condition over other things. The more we draw closer to God, the more we desire and prioritize our relationship with Him.

That's why I am saying it is fundamental and very important for someone to fight this, be born again, and know God. This will make him prioritize what is spiritual despite his weaknesses and struggles.

> "For those who live according to the
> flesh set their minds on the things of the
> flesh, but those *who live* according to
> the Spirit, the things of the Spirit."
> (Romans 8:5)

Those who are born again have the desire to live according to the Spirit.

After a believer falls into sin, there is a moment of sorrow that follows and repentance, but also a time in which he realizes how wrong he had done and a desire to never repeat it again. We need to have this kind of zeal even without having the experience of failure, but sometimes, such moments happen to teach us things. That's why we need to approach the problem and the issue violently without mercy or patience. We need to exterminate all the sin and its leftovers. This is how we need to approach it. If you have something on your phone, such as contacts, media, or anything that can remind you of what is wrong or lead you to it, wipe it out. All of it. God looks at our attitude. If we did anything wrong with another person, we need to let them know that it was a mistake, and we are done with it. This is what the Bible tells us – to demolish the sin, to eradicate it by its roots. This is what God told Saul to do when attacking the Amalekites, who were their enemy—to destroy everything without leaving any traces (1 Samuel 15:1-3). The meaning of this passage is that we need to fight spiritually and do the same with sin. This should be our counterattack toward sin. We are not just surviving and protecting ourselves from it; we must oppose and destroy it. Saul, instead, was merciful toward some of the things of that land and didn't finish with them. That was his mistake that brought consequences into his life (1 Samuel 15:10-28).

As we already said, we need to keep in mind that our heart is the one we will be dealing with when fighting this issue. We need to know it. The One who best knows our heart is God. He knows it even better than us. That's why we need to trust Him and seek Him so that we can be aware of the dangers lying in front of us.

The Bible says in Jeremiah:

> "The heart *is* deceitful above all *things,*
> and desperately wicked; who can know
> it?" (Jeremiah 17:9)

Our hearts might often deceive us and lead us to temptation even when we are unaware of it. Here, we are talking about our deepest and most inner desires that could appear and lead to specific actions. We might often like the feeling of being tempted or just to partially see something that tempts us.

This is how our brain feeds itself with dopamine; this is our inner desire, and subconsciously, we know that this is how we can satisfy the rush we feel. While we expose ourselves to these "light" temptations, we don't see or consider that we might slip up and make the matter worse. Our heart will tell us that it is not a sin as it is nothing so explicit, and it might not be, but it will lead us to something more.

At that moment, we don't think that we might fall. I remember when I used to download movies from certain sites (I am talking about ordinary movies), and some ads sometimes popped up, showing explicit content. I even covered my eyes with my hand so that I would not see it, but at times, maybe just for a split second, I saw them. Those images were stuck in my mind afterward.

I was thinking that as I never looked for those images, and that wasn't my intention, and I just went there to download a movie, all is fine. I was mistaken because these images still impacted me even if I didn't intend to look at them. It is not only a question of whether we see something wrong with the purpose of sinning but also of the fact that it affects us.

We might not have sinned intentionally then, but it still damages and pollutes our minds. We are not dirty just because we are in a certain place or witness something; we are polluted because our minds are being contaminated by those things. If this wasn't happening, then there would be nothing wrong with it. But, as we know that our minds and hearts are inclined to think and react in a certain way, then it is wrong.

This concerns all kinds of sins. Certain things could be sinful for some people and not for others. Speaking about pornography is different, though, because we already said that our brains react in a certain way when watching these images. God is not only forbidding sin because He doesn't like it (this, anyway, is one of the main reasons) but also because it harms us. It damages our relationship with Him.

See, God thinks of our good when forbidding sin. Going back to the earlier conversation about me being tempted by the ads popping up on the site I was visiting for movies, I had to change the way I was doing that and not use the same site.

I know that when it happened again when I visited that site another time, even though I was doing it with a different purpose, my heart was beating heavily while I was surfing there, knowing what I might see. Without realizing it, my inner desire was to see if some ad like those would pop up again.

You can see how deceitful the heart might be. Another situation I can recall is when I checked whether some movies were suitable for me and others. I did this while volunteering in a Christian rehab center, and we used to avoid movies with explicit content or sex scenes. Same as Christian parents, for example, try to do for their kids.

I was going through the movies to see if there was something unsuitable, and again, without realizing when I got to some of those scenes, I was tempted. You need to know that my desire was apparently to help other people not to watch something explicit by checking whether the movies were suitable for them. That might have been my initial desire, but again, without realizing the next time I was doing that, I was doing it knowing that I might see something while checking those movies.

By this, we see how tricky the devil is in deceiving us and how deceitful our hearts are, first of all. Even though the images I saw were not very explicit, and the movies I was checking were not porn movies because, especially at that time, I was too fearful to even get close to the idea I might fall—which is good as an attitude. Still, they were enough to make my mind run and to keep going back a couple of times to see them.

I was tempted, and I fell into sin. We mustn't judge sin by its severity and size only, but by what it could provoke. If we look this way at it, it will probably help us to avoid going further into it and falling into greater sins. Remember how Jesus expressed Himself about sin in the sermon on the mount? He said:

> "You have heard that it was said to
> those of old, 'You shall not murder, and
> whoever murders will be in danger of
> the judgment.' But I say to you
> that whoever is angry with his brother
> without a cause shall be in danger of
> the judgment. And whoever says to his
> brother, 'Raca!' shall be in danger of the
> council. But whoever says, 'You fool!'
> shall be in danger of hell fire." (Matthew
> 5:21–22)

> "You have heard that it was said to
> those of old, 'You shall not commit
> adultery.' But I say to you that
> whoever looks at a woman to lust for
> her has already committed adultery with
> her in his heart." (Matthew 5:27–28)

He wasn't judging sin by what was looking so in man's eyes and what is represented outwardly, but by what it could provoke in the heart. In the same way, we need to examine our hearts and see what is tempting us, what could provoke wrong desires and feelings. The way to fight temptation is to pray or to avoid it. We mustn't miss the part of prayer. If we see that we are vulnerable to temptation and don't have the strength to face it, then we need to avoid it.

> "Flee also youthful lusts; but pursue righteousness, faith, love, peace with those who call on the Lord out of a pure heart." (2 Timothy 2:22)

This passage talks about fleeing lust. This means that if we have a chance, we need to avoid temptation. The only exception I can think of is if this temptation has to do with God's will. It means that God sends us to a certain place to accomplish His will, like reaching out to people with the gospel, for example, and we face a temptation there.

I am pretty sure that if God sent us there, it is with a purpose—and that purpose is not to fall into temptation but to accomplish His will. He will surely also give us the strength to overcome it.

This is a different situation, but we need to still examine the purpose for which we do something well, as we can be easily deceived. Our spiritual health and relationship with God are more important, and as soon as we see that something is not right, we need to avoid the particular situation we are in. Sometimes, this is a better option than going boldly and confidently toward temptation without a solid foundation.

As we said, it is up to the situation, though. If it is something that we cannot avoid because it is part of our life or has to do with God's will, then it is different. But it is better anyway to avoid as much as possible than be overconfident.

The Bible tells us in 1 Corinthians 10:12:

> "Therefore let him who thinks he stands
> take heed lest he fall."

It is better to be always aware. With this, I do not mean that we have to live in fear.

If we see that we cannot avoid the thing tempting us for some important reason, then we need to keep praying. Learning to examine our hearts and see what tempts us is a good beginning to start acting upon the situation. It is not just the adult content we are fighting with; this is not the only thing we need to be aware of.

We also need to see what else we might consider less harmful could provoke us. We have to know that if we fall into that, it could also lead to something worse. If, for example, a scene on TV is tempting us and provoking wrong thoughts in our hearts, then we need to avoid it.

Jesus said that whoever looks at a woman and desires her in his heart has sinned. Does this refer to simply seeing a woman? No. Because if it was so, then we had to blindfold our eyes and never look at a woman again, avoiding even a conversation with her. He wasn't referring to that but to the feelings and desires that someone might have for a woman.

Did Jesus specify how the woman had to dress in that particular situation? No. But He just said that whoever desires her has sinned. She might be dressed in a long dress or a swimming suit, but it is not just a matter of that. I am saying this because sometimes we judge sin by how explicit and obvious it is, without examining our hearts in the way we are tempted, what tempts and is sinful for us, and what could provoke our wrong desires.

As we said before, some people are stronger in certain areas, while others are weak and maybe stronger in others. We mustn't think of a sin just by judging it outwardly. Some men might be strong enough to go to the beach and see women dressed in swimming suits, and others not.

We must never think that we are stronger than we are. That's why porn or adultery isn't the only thing we need to consider as sinful. We need to examine our hearts to define this. If I know that going to a particular place where I see a woman who is tempting me to do something wrong, then I need to avoid it if I can.

So, what defines the severity of sin is not its size only or how others see it, but how it affects our hearts. It is there that we need to be clean. As we already mentioned, our subconscious, which is guided by our desires, would desire sin. Our deceitful heart could profit from that and lead us into that sin.

We must be very careful when we fight addiction or even something more rooted in us as a sexual desire. You remember we said before that sexual desire by itself is not something wrong. God has placed it in us. The problem is when it is accomplished in the wrong and sinful way, such as committing adultery or indulging in porn.

God also wants us to feel pleasure but in the right way. That's why when we fight addiction and know it is something strong, we need to fight it at its beginning. We need to cut it before it gets to a point when it will be too difficult for us. We are examining our weaknesses here.

I have a friend who managed to quit alcohol abuse. It is already three years since he has been out of it. He spent four months in a rehabilitation program. He didn't finish the whole program, and when he got out of there, he relapsed once. It was hard for him, but he didn't give up.

He started regularly attending church services and changed all of his surroundings: people he used to meet with before, friends, places where he used to go, and so on. He doesn't even get close to a bar. He has become an extremist about it. Today, he hasn't touched a drink for almost three years. I am not saying we need to do exactly the same thing to quit our addiction, but we must consider this example.

He is a man who acknowledges his weaknesses and vulnerabilities and wants to do his best for himself and his family. He could have also given up after he relapsed once, but he didn't. He kept on fighting. This is what we need to do, and we need to do it with the help of the Lord.

This effort, together with seeking God and His strength, will help us stand firm. The point is also to understand that what we have been doing is wrong, and we have been at fault when doing it. Sometimes, the consequences that certain addiction has brought in the life of someone could convince him it is wrong, but this is not all.

There are people who have been hurting loved ones, parents, spouses, and children. Some even lost their families. However, we mustn't necessarily get to such a point to be able to understand the gravity of our problem. Sometimes, even looking at what someone has lost cannot help him completely realize that his addiction is something he needs to stay away from.

This is where the gospel plays its part. We need God to convince us that what we have been doing is really wrong. He is the one who can convince us of sin. This helps me greatly in staying away from what is wrong.

Still, once we know clearly what is wrong, we need to know our weak points and understand that our own hearts might deceive us in this case—like my situation when I was going through those movies to check if something was wrong with them. I was doing it for good, to prevent others from seeing what was wrong, but in the end, I was the one tempted.

We need to come quickly to the realization of when we are being deceived. We need to examine ourselves. I am just giving these random examples to show that sometimes it might be too easy for us to be deceived.

You might live in different situations and be tempted by different things. Each of us is weak in a certain area in our life; in those areas, we need to be watchful and alert and build our stronghold there.

> "Keep your heart with all diligence, for
> out of it *spring* the issues of life."
> (Proverbs 4:23)

We must keep our heart above all because it is the most vulnerable and deceitful. Out of it come wrong desires that lead us to take the wrong actions.

Practical Advice Summary

What Can We Do That Can Help Us on the Way?

1. Trust in the Lord.

2. Acknowledge your weakness and vulnerability. We all have it at some point.

3. Seek help from a friend or a close person whom you trust and who understands your problem.

4. Reduce using or delete completely apps and sites that could trigger, awaken, and remind us of sexual desires.

5. Place an adult blocker on your devices.

6. Never give up. Repent. Keep on fighting and see how to improve after failing instead of discouraging yourself.

Chapter 3

Spiritual Health

Sometimes, when we face a temptation, it looks like we cannot make it, that we are overwhelmed, and that we will give in and fall. This is the first impression, though. We need to know that it is always our choice to do it or not, and we will not fall into it until we take action to do it.

When the temptation is present in front of us, it is not over. What will happen next depends entirely on our actions toward it. The advice I am giving is for those who believe, even though it might be practical for everyone. I am saying this to the believers because I know they know the reason why they mustn't fall into sin. They believe in Christ, and along with the reason that falling into porn addiction brings serious consequences, their main reason is that they don't want to hurt His heart and lose their relationship with Him.

Some of this book's directions and advice could also be useful to nonbelievers. Each one needs to decide for himself whether or not to follow Christ. I am just saying that being a believer has benefits in many areas of our lives. We must also know that we don't believe in Christ just for the benefits this relationship brings or just to quit an addiction but for a greater purpose.

Believers are also vulnerable to temptation, as they might not always be strong but at least know the reason to escape it. They do that for God. Other people who also live in a religious environment but don't do it because of God can survive for some time doing it for their own satisfaction or for someone else. Still, these reasons are not valuable enough to help them always resist temptation.

As I was saying, a temptation sometimes might be really strong, and it can look like there is no way to resist it. Still, when we resist it, we see that after that, we don't feel the same desire and rush to do it anymore. When the desire comes, sometimes it looks like there is no other solution to stop feeling it besides fulfilling it. Still, I saw many times when I resisted it, I felt fine afterward, and I even saw God rewarding me in a way. I felt spiritually strong again without a trace of the temptation I felt yesterday.

I am saying this to let you know that God's desire when we face a sin is for us to resist it. There is a way for that. We can also fall into temptation and sin, but we will feel the consequences. There will be time for healing needed and situations we will have to deal with.

How many blessings instead can we have when we resist it? When we resist and don't give in to temptation, we avoid the part where we have to heal, recover, and face the consequences coming after it. I am not talking of condemnation here; I am just saying that we can live fully for God and avoid some consequences that will cause tough moments in life.

Will the believer who has sinned experience blessings and be used for the Lord if he repents? Yes, of course, but he will experience various headaches and trials. A verse in Psalm 51 describes the way David was asking for forgiveness from the Lord after he sinned by committing adultery with Bathsheba.

> "Restore to me the joy of Your
> salvation, and uphold me *by*
> *Your* generous Spirit. *Then* I will teach
> transgressors Your ways, and sinners
> shall be converted to You." (Psalm
> 51:12–13)

With this verse, the psalmist was praying to God to restore Him and was saying that then he was going to teach transgressors God's ways. Notice that he wanted to be restored and, after that, teach others the Lord's way. He wouldn't have done it without being first forgiven and restored. This indicates that he didn't intend to carry on in the sin. After being restored, he was going to teach others. This is our duty as believers, but we cannot perform it when we persevere in sin. This shows us that even after falling into sin, a believer can still be used by God and blessed (if he repents), but it is still a better option to resist it.

If we want to live a Christian life and be blessed by God, we need to have the desire to, at some point, resist sin. We cannot carry on forever with it. If we fail, we need to be restored. God offers us forgiveness. Then, we need to learn to fight it. Throughout the word of God, we see this message.

The word of God doesn't deny the fact that we can find forgiveness when we repent (1 John 1:9), but it never tells us that it is fine or excuses it, letting us think that we can lower our guard in front of temptation.

> "Do not be wise in your own eyes; fear
> the Lord and depart from evil.
> It will be health to your flesh,
> and strength to your bones." (Proverbs
> 3:7–8)

We see here that fearing the Lord is health to our flesh and strength to our bones. We can conclude that the opposite—not fearing and surrendering to sin—will also bring the opposite effects. It means that we will be ill. This illness is not necessarily represented physically.

We can talk a lot about this argument, as sometimes a physical illness could be a trial we are going through, and there are God-fearing Christians who suffer from illness. Here, we are talking about spiritual illness and feeling spiritually down. The Bible tells us not to grieve the Holy Spirit (Ephesians 4:30). Whoever is a believer would know what we are talking about. Just as with physical illness, the same happens with spiritual illness. We would need "time to recover." The more we sin, we can just make the situation worse, and I am not condemning anyone here. I am not saying that God doesn't forgive when we sin or that there is a condemnation; on the contrary, healing and recovering is a beautiful process, but there are consequences. God wants us to avoid them.

When a child burns himself on the stove, for which his father warned him numerous times not to touch it, it eventually heals, but time is needed. And more than this, sometimes he can burn himself so badly that he gets permanent scars. It will heal, but the marks will remain.

This means that it is not meant for us to fall into sin when we face it. Someone might think that as God makes all things work together for good to those who love Him, then we can sin—but it is not in this way. We might've had an experience when things worked for good after we sinned, but this is only because of God's mercies. There is a passage saying:

> "And *why* not *say,* "Let us do evil that
> good may come"?—as we are

> slanderously reported and as some
> affirm that we say. Their condemnation
> is just." (Romans 3:8)

This is what people might think about sinning. But it is not to be taken this way.

> "What shall we say then? Shall we
> continue in sin that grace may
> abound? Certainly not! How shall we
> who died to sin live any longer in it?"
> (Romans 6:1–2)

We can see some examples in the Bible. David sinned with Bathsheba, and the Lord forgave him, but afterward, a kind of judgment came upon him. There is judgment coming into the believer's life while in this life. To the rest of the people, and I am referring to nonbelievers here, it will happen after this life. After sinning (and repenting), David's firstborn from that relationship died. And after some time, his son Absalom rose against him (2 Samuel 15).

Yes, God made things work out for good because David received forgiveness and was restored, and the second child he had from that relationship was Solomon, who later on became a king and the wisest man on earth. Still, there were consequences of David's sinful relationship with Bathsheba. Consequences happen with the purpose of letting us learn a lesson so that we can avoid sinning the next time. One of the natural consequences sin brings is death.

> "For the wages of sin *is* death, but the
> gift of God *is* eternal life in Christ Jesus
> our Lord." (Romans 6:23)

In order to avoid these consequences, God warns us and corrects our lives when needed. All of this is so that we can avoid death. By this, we see that God is good when He corrects His sons. This is with the purpose that we can be disciplined.

Sometimes, it might be painful, but our Father loves us, and He prefers to let us feel a bit of pain now through which we can learn rather than not letting us feel anything and die and be judged on the final day.

The same happened with Samson. He sinned by letting his secret be known to Delilah (he first made a mistake by becoming involved with her). Afterward, he was blinded and enslaved by his enemies, the Philistines. We all know from the story that in the end, even though blinded and enslaved, Samson prayed to God, and he managed to defeat more enemies than ever before in his life. Yes, we again see that God made all things work out for good, but what consequences did he go through!

Let's see some other practical examples of life. There is a situation that I can recall. I remember when I once fell into a sin. Straight after that, my pastor, without knowing that, invited me to deliver a message on

Sunday in front of the whole congregation. I thought thoroughly about it, and I had to be sincere with myself and deny the invitation. I am not saying that this applies to all cases, and I am not saying either that God cannot use us if we sin and we repent, but teaching the word of God and leading a congregation is a huge responsibility, and I had to be sincere.

I just didn't feel that I measured up, and I explained the situation to my pastor and why I denied the invitation. Being sincere with ourselves and the people surrounding us is also something that will help us in healing and overcoming the issue of porn and any other sin.

Sometimes, it is better to be a mess but true than to look perfect but be false at the same time. I know this might cost us, and we might have a reputation, but most important is our reputation in front of God.

Let's look at another practical example. Imagine a pastor who is having a good, godly ministry in a great church. Let's say he stumbles and commits adultery, for example. Many times, even if we don't confess specific sins, they cannot remain hidden for a long time as God brings things to light.

Same as the case in King David's life. What happens in most ministries is that the pastor will be dismissed from his ministry and will likely never return to his position. Even if no one caught him, he should be sincere enough to admit his faults. Of course, God forgives and restores, and He will raise that person again from the ashes, but how many troubles and consequences could be avoided if he never made certain mistakes?

For those who have already done something wrong and now desire to rise again, I say that God has preordained something amazing for them ahead, and they must be encouraged and carry on the road. Time cannot be rewound. Whatever happened is in the past. We need to learn from our mistakes, ask for forgiveness, and carry on.

In a later stage, our experiences could serve someone else who will be in our situation. I am saying this as a warning for future experiences. Is God going to forgive the pastor who sinned in a drastic way? Yes, if he is a real believer, he will repent and be restored, but he might lose his ministry and blessings, such as teaching and leading his congregation.

Chapter 4

How Do We Face Temptation?

In some of the previous chapters, we discussed how we can avoid temptation. Nevertheless, temptation is something that will come no matter what. The world in which we live, especially today, is this way.

How do we need to face the temptation once it is at our door? Below, you will find a reflection showing the spiritual side and God's way of facing temptation. You can find some practical advice in this book that could be applied by people who don't believe in God, and it can be helpful to them. However, this is one of the chapters more focused on the way God wants to help us when facing temptation.

I cannot force anyone to change his opinion or become a Christian, but I can tell you that some—and even most—times, we don't have a way to fight our addictions. There is strength and power that can be found only in God.

The Bible says in James 4:7:

"Therefore submit to God. Resist the
devil and he will flee from you."

This verse indicates that the devil will flee from us. I think he will indeed not flee because of us and because he is confronted with *us*, but because we have submitted to God. The devil is the one who brings temptations into our lives. We are the ones who fall into them, but what are we supposed to do when facing one?

As believers, we often know that they are wrong; we know what is correct and tend to prevent falling into them with our own strength. But this is not enough. We may try for a while an attempt to escape temptation and resist it with our strength, but sooner or later, we discover that we cannot face it in a proper way, and some of those times, when we do it in our way, we see that we fail. Then, we start to examine where we made a mistake and what we lacked; we begin to condemn ourselves, to think that we love sin more than God.

There are so many consequences because of sin. Consequences that come into our lives because we fell into them. But in the end, it's much better if we avoid falling into them. So, how can we properly face them?

In the verse we read before, we said that we must first submit to God, then resist the devil, and he will flee from us. How do we submit to God? By having a relationship with Him. So, when that sin comes knocking on our doors, we need to resist him by having a relationship with God and trusting Him to fight that sin.

How many times have we known that and taken it for granted? We thought we already had that power in us, acknowledging, of course, that it is given by God. Yet, we don't realize that this power needs to be maintained in our lives by having a constant relationship with Him. The same is true when, in the Bible, it is said that our lamps must always be kept burning.

> "Then the Lord spoke to Moses, saying:
> "Command the children of Israel that
> they bring to you pure oil of pressed
> olives for the light, *to make the lamps
> burn continually*." (Leviticus 24:1–2,
> emphasis added)

> "Let your waist be girded
> and *your lamps burning*; and you
> yourselves be like men who wait for
> their master, when he will return from
> the wedding, that when he comes and
> knocks they may open to him
> immediately. (Luke 12:35–36, emphasis
> added)

When we take the matter of having His protection and strength in us for granted, we carry on with our strength. Still, the Bible, in many places, tells us to keep praying and reading His word. This means to have a relationship with Him, and I am not talking to nonbelievers here. Of course, this message might be good for them as well. But indeed, we are talking about Christians and believers because they might forget to trust the Lord.

I mean to have a constant relationship with Him. They might still be blessed in some areas of their lives and even used by the Lord in some ways. Of course, when talking about not having a proper relationship with the Lord, I'm not referring exclusively to people not praying, reading, or believing in His words at all. No. I am also talking of people who are born-again believers. They would read the word, pray, and seek the Lord, but occasionally.

He will somehow bless their lives, but still, they will lack in this area of their lives, which will bring consequences. There are believers who because of everyday busyness and doings, might have this attitude and occasionally be involved in the Lord's work. Don't say: Okay, today is Sunday service anyway; I will not have my devotional time with His word in the morning, as I will listen to it in the service anyway. Or, tomorrow is another day, now I need to keep busy with something else.

I'm not saying this for condemnation; I'm just saying it so that we believers can be awakened and edified. I am also placing myself in this group. Often, I have difficulty focusing on my relationship with the Lord.

Why am I not going to God even when a temptation or other crucial moment comes?

I know the law of God. I know what is right and wrong and want to follow the right path. I should pray as the first thing when facing a difficult situation or a temptation, but I don't. Why? Because I am probably not so used to that, and I haven't built my relationship with the Lord.

Sometimes, we consider the Christian life as keeping certain laws and doing what is right, which is a part of it, but we don't see it as a relationship with the Lord. Instead, this should be the main thing and help us do the rest.

We might know the law, know what is right and what is not, and try to resist the temptation with our own strength, but we will eventually end up suffering because those things are much stronger than us. And imagine if the devil is directly involved with that temptation. We know he is mainly involved in those situations.

Many times, it is also true that we're the ones who tempt ourselves. We are the ones who take the steps, but he is always there present at the moment. When the devil tempts us, we are the ones who open the doors of our hearts to him, and he takes advantage of the situation.

Some people give up because they just don't care about falling into temptation, and fighting it doesn't have value for them. Others do it because they don't have enough strength to resist it. The truth is that none of us has, but that's why the Grace of God is needed. Grace is not only needed to forgive our sins but also to empower us to live a godly life (2 Peter 1:2–3).

For those who want to resist and fight temptations, I have to say that the devil is so much stronger and smarter than all of us. He is not somebody with whom we can play or make jokes. We also know that no temptation that is too strong will come to us, and God will not allow us to be tempted beyond what we are able to bear.

> "Therefore let him who thinks he stands
> take heed lest he fall. No temptation
> has overtaken you except such as is
> common to man;
> but God *is* faithful, who will not allow
> you to be tempted beyond what you are
> able, but with the temptation will also
> make the way of escape, that you may
> be able to bear *it.*" (1 Corinthians 10:13)

By this verse, it seems that we can overcome all temptations coming in front of us, and this, in part, should encourage us to believe that the Lord doesn't want us to fall into temptations and that He is willing to help us. Where is the problem, then? Where is the problem when someone falls? In one of the phrases of our Father's prayer in Matthew 6:9–13, it is said:

"And do not lead us Into temptation, but
deliver us from the evil one."

What does "And do not lead us into temptation" mean? We all know that the Lord is sovereign. Our steps depend on Him. In the Bible, it is even said that man does not direct his own steps (Proverbs 16:9). Does this mean that we are led to sin and will fall into it anyway? Not at all. Because, on the other hand, He requires from us not to fall into it and not to live sinful lifestyles. He wants us to be saved.

The Bible also says that He gave certain people up to vile passions because they did not glorify Him as God (Romans 1:21–25). This is what I think the passage of Matthew 6:13 means. He is preventing us from getting into a temptation we cannot stand. But if He is not with us, and we are given up to our own passions, as it is said in Romans 1:24, we are exposed to temptations we cannot stand at. All we have to do is to be with Him.

Then, the passage in 1 Corinthians 10:13, which says that God will not allow us to be tempted beyond our limits, takes place. In the story of Job, we see that God was the One, allowing things to happen in the life of Job. It was because the devil asked for those things, but God had the final say. I am sure that if God allowed the devil to do whatever he wanted, Job wouldn't be alive.

But there was a plan for the life of Job, and God did not allow for him to be tested beyond what he could handle. Therefore, we see that the best option is to be on God's side. Then He will protect us from falling far from Him, and whatever happens will be for our good. Otherwise, we will be given up to our sinful desires, and the devil will do whatever he wants with us. The verse before 1 Corinthians 10:13, which says that God will not allow us to be tempted beyond what we can bear, states:

> "Therefore let him who thinks he stands
> take heed lest he fall." (1 Corinthians
> 10:12)

This means we can fall if we think we stand and are too confident in ourselves. Pride is also a reason to be far from God. If we stick with Him, He will not lead us into temptation. God is sovereign, and we cannot change or control this, but if we are with Him, He will not lead us into temptation.

This is what we have to pray for! We pray for something we cannot achieve by ourselves. We need God to do that. He is all-powerful and sovereign. It means that we cannot excuse ourselves with the fact that He is sovereign, but that we need rather to trust in Him, as it depends on Him. He is greater than anything else.

This matter is serious and very important in our lives, and we need to take these issues seriously. How can we defeat the devil who is much stronger and smarter than us? By asking for help from someone stronger than him. That's why when the Bible tells us always to pray (1 Thessalonians 5:16–18), it is for a reason. This is so fundamental. Jesus was always praying. He gave us a perfect example of that. It is important that we train ourselves to practice it.

Sometimes, it is not a matter if we have or don't have the desire to pray or read the Word; we just need to do it. This should be a customary practice. Of course, we mustn't do it for the sake of doing it only or to do it to feel better and to say, "I've done what I was supposed to." No. We do that because we acknowledge our weaknesses and need His strength.

And if we sometimes don't find an answer straight away, we need to keep doing it until we do. Do you remember the parable of the unjust judge and the widow who was asking him for justice (Luke 18:1–5)? This is how we need to be persistent.

When we talk about being constant, it is not just a matter of blindly persisting but also examining ourselves and praying to the Lord to help us change our attitude and have more faith. The fact that sometimes He might not be answering us when we ask Him for something might indicate that there is something wrong. I'm not saying that we have sinned in something particular, even if this might be the case, but I'm saying that we might have doubted or lacked forgiveness.

It might be for this or other reasons; we need to examine ourselves. I'm not pointing out or saying what exactly your problem might be; I am just suggesting. I'm saying that when we pray and see something is not answered, this could be due to the time we are going through because the Lord probably has reserved things for us—but we will have them in His time.

Still, some of the reasons we do not receive something might be because of something else that needs to be sorted out in our lives. I am also not necessarily talking about something particular we're asking for. We might just ask to see God and desire His presence and blessings in our lives.

When we see that we don't receive an answer, we start to examine ourselves to see if there is any situation or even a hidden sin that we don't know of. This is also how the Lord shows us and sheds light in our hearts so we can change that—by passing through a desert where we don't have a clear answer many times and where our hearts are tested.

We change those things we find out in us by going to Him with them. Someone might be asking, "Why is it that He doesn't just change that in us without going through this process?" He could do that, of course, but the reason why we need to go through a desert, a trial, and we need to discover and see our sin *is because this makes us humble. This attitude is the one that pleases the Lord most.*

"And you shall remember that
the Lord your God led you all the way
these forty years in the wilderness, to
humble you *and* test you, to know
what *was* in your heart, whether you
would keep His commandments or not."
(Deuteronomy 8:2)

This verse talks about the reason He led His nation, Israel, to go through a desert.

Often, God speaks to us while we go through a desert. On the contrary, we are inclined to think that the better we feel, the closer to God we are, and we will hear more His voice. It is not always this way. We can even say that sometimes these are not the conditions to have a deeper relationship with Him. In Hosea 2:14, it is said:

"Therefore, behold, I will allure her, will
bring her into the wilderness,
and speak comfort to her."

Here, God compares His nation, Israel, to an unfaithful woman because instead of following, serving, and loving Him, they went after other foreign gods and idols. When we fall into sin and temptation and keep doing it, we are like that unfaithful woman. This example is for us as well. As she was unfaithful, He decided to take her to the desert, where He would talk to her.

God uses these moments where He allows us to go through a trial, lets us see our sins, and then talks to us. A desert could not necessarily be for what we only esteem as sinful but also for things we need to discover in our hearts or to find a deeper relationship with God. The Bible gives a good example regarding getting in-depth with God:

> 46 "But why do you call Me 'Lord, Lord,'
> and not do the things which I
> say? 47 Whoever comes to Me, and
> hears My sayings and does them, I will
> show you whom he is like: 48 He is like a
> man building a house, *who dug deep*
> *and laid the foundation on the rock*. And
> when the flood arose, the stream beat
> vehemently against that house, and
> could not shake it, for it was [i]founded
> on the rock. 49 But he who heard and
> did nothing is like a man who built a
> house on the earth without a
> foundation, against which the stream
> beat vehemently; and immediately it fell.
> And the ruin of that house was great."
> (Luke 6:46–49, emphasis added)

This is the example of the man who built his house on the rock. We know that the rock is Jesus. It is said that he dug deep in the ground to find the rock. So, we conclude that going through trials and a desert is good because it helps us examine ourselves and get deeper into God.

The parable of the house on the rock also tells us that we need to dig deeper so that we can find a foundation. It is good at the beginning of someone's life when he finds the rock, and it is also good afterward, as each person needs to examine himself from time to time.

So, when we go through a spiritual drought, we must persevere and examine what this is for. The Lord doesn't delay. He will actually show up and answer us. The Book of Psalms contains many such cases, where we read about people crying day and night to the Lord without having a clear answer. So, what is important is to have the practice of praying and looking for answers from the Lord, even if we don't always find them immediately.

I'm saying this to those who have been born again and have a relationship with the Lord. When we convert to Him, Heaven's gates are open to us. We have an entrance to heaven. The matter is that sometimes we're not using it. Praying is not a gift. It is not like one of those unique gifts given to you for a specific purpose, and it is not some kind of charisma.

Of course, there will be people more dedicated to it, but this is something asked of all Christians and believers. There's no exception. So, this is how we can defeat temptation. What is most important and what the Christian faith is built on is God and our relationship with Him.

The Christian faith is not built on the fact that we are righteous and keep the law. You mustn't misunderstand me here. Of course, this is part of it, but our relationship with the Lord is essential. We love God because we know Him.

It is the same as knowing a person. We know that person because we have a relationship with him. Because we talk with him, we know what he likes or dislikes. We can often build an image of someone in our minds, which might be the wrong image. This changes when we start having conversations and communion with that person.

This relationship and communion with Jesus are expressed in having Him as a friend, starting our day by praising Him and asking Him to accompany us. This mustn't be done only when we are in a particular need. What God desires for us is different. He sees and examines our hearts and knows when we want to use Him just to sort out our situations and personal issues. This also determines if our prayers will be answered.

In the same way, we mustn't look for God only when we see we are in front of temptation. We need to have done that before that moment arrives. We often want just the final product; we want the blessing of the relationship with God. Imagine if you have a friend and look to be with that friend only when you are in need.

Indeed, friends are there to help us, but what would he think if you looked for him only in those moments?

Instead, we need to maintain that relationship at any moment. This is fundamental because, in heaven, we will have a perfect relationship with Him. Still, it needs to start from here. If we see that we don't have that natural desire to draw to God and look for Him at any moment, and not only when we are in trouble, we need to ask Him to help us develop that kind of special relationship. Because this is what is really important—to love Him. This is also the first commandment.

> "Jesus said to him, "'You shall love
> the Lord your God with all your heart,
> with all your soul, and with all your
> mind.' This is *the* first and great
> commandment." (Matthew 22:37–38)

This is what He desires for us. His love helps us develop that relationship. The more we know about His love and experience His mercy, the more we will love Him and our neighbor. This kind of relationship is a foundation for our lives. Often, a Christian life could seem like just following and keeping commandments, doing what is right, and avoiding what is wrong, but this is a part of it; it is not all.

Many people can do what is right for personal gratification, while in the Christian life, the focus doesn't turn around us, but around God. We must do what is right in front of Him and for Him. When we accept and comprehend it, and even when we don't comprehend it sometimes. When our main focus is just about observing the commandments, and we do it for ourselves only, then when the time comes to really walk in them and practice them, we see that we don't possess the power to do that.

When instead, we have the attitude to walk in them for Him because we love Him and fear Him; we develop a relationship with Him and succeed. I am not saying that Christians, even those maintaining a relationship with God, don't fail or sin. We all sin, but the difference is in the capability we receive from Him to avoid that happening frequently and to rise after we fall. Sometimes, the difference might also be in the kind of sin.

Christianity could turn into a practice of insensitively observing the commandments for personal gratification, also for those who know God and are born again. We can even say that it could be a common occurrence. Apostle Paul wrote something about this in 1 Corinthians 3:10–15:

> 10 According to the grace of God which was given to me, as a wise master builder I have laid the foundation, and another builds on it. But let each one take heed how he builds on it. 11 For no other foundation can anyone lay than that which is laid, which is Jesus

Christic. [12] Now if anyone builds on this foundation *with* gold, silver, precious stones, wood, hay, straw, [13] each one's work will become clear; for the Day will declare it, because it will be revealed by fire; and the fire will test each one's work, of what sort it is. [14] If anyone's work which he has built on *it* endures, he will receive a reward. [15] If anyone's work is burned, he will suffer loss; but he himself will be saved, yet so as through fire.

Here, it is indicated that even though believers have the same foundation, they could build on it with different materials. To me, this has to do with the way a believer lives. Some people might have found Christ and repented, but they still will not be as dedicated as others.

We all need to have a foundation, but how we will build on it and which materials we will use is up to us. This matter depends on our relationship with the Lord. It depends on our holiness as well. We are all weak in our flesh, but if we are always falling into sins and not taking the issue seriously, it also means that we probably build with straw or wood, which are materials that do not endure fire. This means that the Bible encourages us to make an effort, and aim in a way to be better in our relationship with God and be closer to Him.

Sometimes, people might be looking just for the blessing the Christian life can bring to someone. Also, believers could focus more on that and pray for it. While this is not wrong by itself, we need to know that the Giver of the blessings is much more important than the blessings themselves and the things He can provide. He even says in His word:

> "But seek first the kingdom of God and
> His righteousness, and all these things
> shall be added to you." (Matthew 6:33)

This indicates that we need first to glorify Him because this is what the Kingdom of Heaven is about— glorifying God and seeking Him first. Then, it is said that all the rest shall be added. It is even said that our prayer mustn't be focused mainly on that—for the things of this life.

It is not that we mustn't pray at all, but it is said that the heathen (people who do not know God) look for those things first. This is also what He was referring to when saying that they make vain repetitions:

> "And when you pray, do not use vain
> repetitions as the heathen *do*. For they
> think that they will be heard for their
> many words. "Therefore do not be like
> them. For your Father knows the things
> you have need of before you ask
> Him." (Matthew 6:7)

Straight after saying that we mustn't use vain repetitions, He says that our Father knows what we need before asking Him. I think He was referring to the things we use, the things we sometimes esteem as blessings but are just part of what we need to live everyday life.

This means we can pray occasionally for what we need—food, clothing, etc., but it mustn't be our main focus when praying. Our main petition should be about what glorifies God. Pure life, for example, pleasing God and having Him in the first place, glorifies Him. This is one of the things I should be praying for.

At times, I could pray to the Lord to give me a godly spouse, but this should be done at times because it falls under the things that shall be added to me. Having a pure life should instead be one of my main and daily petitions.

When we focus on looking for the Lord for certain blessings only, it happens that when a trial comes, and we want to be delivered, it doesn't happen because we haven't truly looked for Him before that. We only looked for Him at the moment when trouble or temptation came into our lives. He knows the attitude of our hearts.

We want to be blessed and delivered during trials and tough moments. We also want to be used by the Lord. We think of all the things we've left behind and surrendered, believing that the Lord should answer our petitions because of that. In this way, we make it sound like it is by the works we've done, while the Bible explicitly says that it is by faith, meaning that we need to have a relationship with Him and believe in Him.

There are some practical examples in the Bible where we see how people looked more for what the Lord could provide. I mean, they looked more for their commodity and material needs than the spiritual blessings and Him. They didn't have faith in Him. This happened to the Israelites in the desert.

> [1]Moreover, brethren, I do not want you to be unaware that all our fathers were under the cloud, all passed through the sea, [2] all were baptized into Moses in the cloud and in the sea, [3] all ate the same spiritual food, [4] and all drank the same spiritual drink. For they drank of that spiritual Rock that followed them, and that Rock was Christ. [5] But with most of them God was not well pleased, for *their bodies* were scattered in the wilderness.
>
> [6] Now these things became our examples, to the intent that we should not lust after evil things as they also lusted. [7] And do not become idolaters as *were* some of them. As it is written, "The people sat down to eat

and drink, and rose up to play." [8] Nor let us commit sexual immorality, as some of them did, and in one day twenty-three thousand fell; [9] nor let us tempt Christ, as some of them also tempted, and were destroyed by serpents; [10] nor complain, as some of them also complained, and were destroyed by the destroyer. [11] Now all these things happened to them as examples, and they were written for our admonition, upon whom the ends of the ages have come. (1 Corinthians 10:1–11)

This passage talks of the nation of Israel, who were going through the desert, and it says that all of them passed through the sea and were baptized in Moses, in the cloud, and in the sea, and ate spiritual food. This indicates they had experiences with God, and we can compare them with today's believers. Yet, it is said that God wasn't pleased with all of them because while going through the desert, they complained, fell into idol worship, and committed sexual immorality.

This means it is not enough to be a believer and have repented once upon a time. I think they lacked faith and didn't develop it because they didn't have a proper relationship with God. We can see they were looking and complaining mostly about what is material, like food and water, things that I think God was going to provide for them anyway. They focused more on what God could provide for them than God Himself and His promises.

As we already mentioned, we often want to develop a relationship with God and trust in Him only in times of need or when we have already fallen into temptation. Having a life free of chains and addictions is built on the fact that we avoid falling into them much before they come.

We are not striving to pursue a better relationship with God and grow in faith only when we fall, but even when we haven't fallen and are not in danger. It is to say that we are not seeking God only to be addiction-free but primarily because we love Him.

Even though we know the scripture in Romans 8:28, saying: "And we know that all things work together for good to those who love God, to those who are the called according to *His* purpose." it is not something that we can lean on when facing temptation—it is of a great treasure and help while we recover after falling.

It would be of great help if we understood the context in which it was written. It is a scripture for those who believe in God and fear Him. It is for those who want to please Him, and even though they didn't want to, they failed God somehow.

When this happens to a spiritual person, he becomes sorrowful, not only for the consequences coming from that sin but because he hurt the heart of God. Many people could become sorrowful because they lost some things, such as a job, position, or dignity, but not all feel bad because they sinned in front of God.

One of the purposes of the scripture in Romans 8:28, however, is to encourage godly people who go through trials or seek God's help after failing Him in a certain area of their lives. The following scriptures speak of how godly people feel after failing God (Psalm 51, Psalm 32:3–5, Matthew 26:75).

> 3 When I kept silent, my bones grew old
> Through my groaning all the day long.
> 4 For day and night Your hand was
> heavy upon me;
> My vitality was turned into the drought
> of summer. *Selah*
> 5 I acknowledged my sin to You,
> And my iniquity I have not hidden.
> I said, "I will confess my transgressions
> to the Lord,"
> And You forgave the iniquity of my
> sin. *Selah* (Psalm 32:3–5)

This psalm describes how a believer feels when sinning. Surely, the people living those experiences didn't take some of the promises of God as a way to excuse themselves or hear someone saying to them:

"Don't worry, all is fine. There is no condemnation for those who are in Christ."

Even when believers know these promises or hear them from someone, they don't take matters lightly. They know how they feel. Even when they feel comforted by God and His promises, they went through sorrow before that.

The entire chapter of Romans 8 talks about consolation and comfort for believers. There are scriptures such as:

> "*There is* therefore now no condemnation to those who are in Christ Jesus, who do not walk according to the flesh, but according to the Spirit." (Romans 8:1)

> "And we know that all things work together for good to those who love God, to those who are the called according to *His* purpose." (Romans 8:28)

> "What then shall we say to these things? If God *is* for us, who *can be* against us?" (Romans 8:31)

Those scriptures contain very valuable promises and are encouraging. We have to emphasize that the scriptures mentioned above, encourage those who are afflicted and sorrowful for what they have done, and they don't use them as an excuse to sin.

The Bible doesn't just talk of unlimited joy, happiness, and success. These are things we could achieve in this life, and God can help us with that, but there is also sorrow, and Jesus said, "Blessed *are* those who mourn, for they shall be comforted." (Matthew 5:4)

However, when we trust in God and take His promises seriously, even when we fall into sin, we learn something from it—and even if the experience is painful, we become better persons after that. By "better persons," I mean persons who draw closer to God. I can see it in my life, too. Each time something wrong happened to me or I failed God, I learned from it. In this way, I could better see my weak points. This made me more humble and not so confident in myself.

I don't know, but it's possible that this prevented me from making an even bigger mistake afterward. Only God knows that. We cannot, however, say this each time we fall, but we need to trust God. In this way, when we love God and we take matters in the right way, the passage in Romans 8:28, saying that all things work together for good to those who love God, takes place.

Speaking about the true believers, it is not a question that God cannot forgive us. He forgives. He is faithful. Yet, He tells us not to sin anymore (John 8:11). Sometimes, by keeping on sinning, we can let negative thoughts come into us, and we give space to the devil to attack our faith. Then, we need to really have strong faith to rise up.

Still, with porn, it is not the same as with other sins. It is not like telling a lie, for example, or getting angry with someone. These are things for which we will get sorrowful, and we will repent if we are God-fearing people. When we fall into porn, we can also find forgiveness if we are Christians. The problem is that it creates an addiction, and after each instance of backsliding, we are prompted to fall again, and there is a risk of repeating it as the addiction will pull us into it. This is true with all kinds of addictions. When it starts happening more often, we give more space to the devil, and we can easily get weaker in faith. When sinning repeatedly, we risk hardening our hearts.

Other sins are different, as they cannot become as addictive as this one, and we can fight them more easily for this reason. When we engage with porn, we start craving the images and the rush they provoke in our minds. With time, those who are addicted to adult content start desiring more of it.

It happens exactly the same as with any other drug. When the brain and the body develop a tolerance to a certain dose, they start craving more of it. Those who are addicted to porn start desiring more of it or looking for more explicit content. Sometimes, it is not the sexual desire a person is having that needs to be satisfied but the rush they feel when engaging with adult content.

This is clearly an addiction. It perverts our perspective on sexual acts. That's why even married people can get hooked on it. I personally know what an addiction is because I was a heroin addict in the past. I was delivered, thanks to God. After a while, when I had to deal with adult content, I was surprised and scared at the same time. I discovered the same kind of addiction that drugs were producing in me before. I knew I had to cut off what I was doing and rise with the Lord's help.

Chapter 5

Rising Up and Healing

What is important is that we can know how to rise in a proper way after we fail. The way we recover is very important and will define what will happen next in most cases. We may feel really down after we relapse. We may feel worthless and think there is no sense in continuing to fight and just wishing to rewind time.

This cannot be done, however. Whatever happened, happened, and we have to make the best of each situation, no matter how absurd this may sound. We may see it as a total failure, but still, we need to get the best out of it. This will happen if we are believers, and we love and seek God. Only believers are able to draw good out of what is bad (Romans 8:28). Then, even the problem and the trials will be for our good. This, however, doesn't allow us to sin and not to be careful.

Yes, we may feel worthless after failing, but we need to take this frustration to God. In some cases, the answer is not to forget all that is negative and think positively. Instead, we need to take what we feel negatively to God. This will help us to repent in a genuine way. Some people keep the frustration, and in this way, they give up fighting, as they are not strong enough to bear it. No one is.

Some others might just try to forget about it. This is not the way, either. God says in His word that He is faithful and will forgive us if we confess our sins and we repent:

> "If we confess our sins, He is faithful
> and just to forgive us *our* sins and
> to cleanse us from all unrighteousness."
> (John 1:9)

This passage should encourage us and let us run to God when something is wrong. If we feel discouraged after sinning, it means that we are from the group of people that love the heart of God and don't want to displease Him. This discouragement, though, mustn't turn into giving up and saying, "It happened again. I just can't make it. There is no solution."

On the contrary, this discouragement and feeling down need to encourage us to go to God. There are people who don't feel at all discouraged when sinning and take it as something normal. This is a worse condition, but we also need to be careful not to get discouraged from carrying on forward because of our failure.

We need to know that God is waiting for us to come to Him. Yes, He will correct us as each father corrects his child when doing something wrong, but He is waiting for us to accept us and receive us after we fail. That's why there are various passages in the Bible inviting us to go to Him when feeling this way. He receives us. The passage in Hebrews 4:16 is one of them.

> "Let us therefore come boldly to the
> throne of grace, that we may obtain
> mercy and find grace to help in time of
> need."

After realizing the wrong we have done and making peace with God, we need to get to the next step— healing. One of the important factors in that process is to realize and really understand how harmful our issues are. I am not talking just about porn, but about any kind of addiction.

It is not just to feel displeased for what we have lost, but to realize how wrong it is the addiction in itself.

> [18] Flee sexual immorality. Every sin that
> a man does is outside the body, but he
> who commits sexual immorality
> sins against his own body. [19] *Or do you*
> *not know that your body is the temple of*
> *the Holy Spirit who is in you, whom you*
> *have from God, and you are not your*
> *own?* [20] For you were bought at a price;
> therefore glorify God in your body and
> in your spirit, which are God's.

This passage has to do with not harming our bodies with substances or any other way, but it also places an emphasis on sexual sin, telling us that it is something wrong.

Trials and hardships during the process of rehabilitation

I'll be giving some examples given by some specialists and doctors dealing with this area of addiction. But, we need to know that when talking of rehabilitation, I am not referring to a specific program, steps, or time (even if time is also needed), but of the quality with which we go through that time and the foundation we build on. This is fundamental.

That's why I do not prefer to use the word "rehabilitation" because when people hear it, they think of a specific program and way of doing things that would help anyone who is undergoing it—but it actually depends on the personal journey and faith each individual has. He, of course, should follow the rules and the advice others give him, and there should also be a certain pattern to follow, but it is a matter of personal faith, effort, and journey.

I will still tell you what the specialists are saying because it is also something that needs to be known and considered so that we can be aware of what we are going to, as this can also help us along the way.

After the realization of what we have done and repentance, there comes the next step—healing. This step requires patience and perseverance. Straight after we fail and repent, which is fundamental, we might go through a time of being in the desert. The desert represents a place where somebody goes through hardships and trials and feels a strong lack of certain things. We are not in our comfort zone when we are in a desert.

The matter is that if we have been involved in some addiction, we are used to providing our comfort and well-being through non-natural and wrong ways. These substances and addictions were making us feel fine but mostly were harming us, too. Now, we need to go from one stage to another where we can feel comfort and satisfaction, not through what could harm us but through what is sound and really good for us.

While stepping out from one stage to the other, we will feel like going through drought, loneliness, and difficulty most of the time. This, though, is a necessary part of healing and changing. Sometimes, this process could take time. We cannot avoid the pain sometimes, even if we would like to. This is for our good.

It is the same with falling into any kind of sin. We don't feel fine straight away afterward. The first stage, if we fear God and if we are believers, is grief. Then we go to God, and we repent. After that, joy comes. Still, grief is a part of the process. The desert is a stage in which we need to be perseverant, patient, and have faith. This stage cannot be avoided, and any attempts we make to avoid it might be harmful. Any way we try to avoid the pain or alleviate it, is not good.

I am not saying that we need to live always in pain, but that we need to go through it. This helps us to realize what caused it, and in this way, we also change. God works in our lives and changes us in two ways sometimes. One is through His glory and presence, where we feel fine and are close to Him, and the other is through a desert and tough times. We are the ones who often cause those tough moments and deserts in our lives, but He uses them, as He is the One who knows how to make things work for our good, even through hardships (Romans 8:28).

The moments we live in His presence, and we are close to Him are also preceded by tough moments. In this way, we learn to appreciate His glory and know Him in a deeper way. So, we see that both these cases—desert trials and His presence and glory—go together.

The moments we live in His glory and we are fine are important, but still, He tells us that also the moments of trials are important and warns us that situations like that will occur in life. We cannot stay on the mountain alone. There is also a valley.

Peter wanted to make tabernacles when he saw Jesus's glory revealed on the mountain. He wanted to remain forever in that glorious moment (Matthew 17:4). Still, this didn't happen, as this is not a moment that is meant to last forever (at least here on earth). We will go through mountaintops and valleys, through ups and downs.

Meditating on this, we need to understand that life is made by good moments, but in most cases, they are not prevalent. We need to get used to the other moments, too. The problem is that when looking only for comfort, which is impossible always to have, we begin looking for it in the wrong way.

This is also part of the addiction. We are looking for the substance or thing that could provide us with that momentary pleasure but without thinking about the consequences afterward. In this way, we avoid facing reality, which is essential to experience, as it may also involve moments of adversity that are good for our growth. In this way, we avoid facing our giants and problems, which, with time, become greater and more uncontrollable. So, when recovering from addiction, we see that we need to go through the sorrow, which in the beginning might be enhanced, but with time, things return to normal.

Same as any other addiction, in the first period, we will feel strong cravings, and we are the most vulnerable. This is when our mind will desire the dopamine dosage it was accustomed to. This is when we need to be very careful, and if we consider applying any restrictions (see Chapter 2), now is the time.

If we discover that there are certain habits and patterns that in themselves are not harmful but can still cause us to relapse, we need to cut them out, too. These restrictions, which might be strong at the beginning, need to be applied at least for a time, even always if that is the case. We need to examine the situation well. There might be certain TV shows we need to avoid, as they could trigger things in us, using our devices at a certain hour, going to certain places, etc.

According to some specialists in the field, *it takes up to 90 days when the addiction is stronger, and that will be the most critical time*. This period is also called the *crisis/decision stage*. Recovering from addiction, however, requires effort and constant awareness. We all need to consider our weak points and be careful there.

Some people say that quitting porn begins at the moment someone turns off his browser. The matter is to persevere in being clean. To be able to do that, a person needs to change radically some of his habits and even his lifestyle. When you are a believer, you have a double motivation to do it because you already want to please God, and you know that He is against addiction and pornography. The Bible explicitly says this in Matthew 5:28:

> "But I say to you that whoever looks at a
> woman to lust for her has already
> committed adultery with her in his
> heart."

The lifestyle promoted in the Bible is about seeking to live in the right way and striving to live a holy life. We know that this is impossible for us. We need God's strength to achieve it. The Bible also teaches us to live an open life and to be in the light without hiding what we are. All these attributes we find in the Bible could help a lot when we fight such a problem.

To be in this position, though, and to be able to fight in such a way, we need to know God and to have had an encounter with Him. The difference between believers and any other ordinary people is that believers know how to rise when they fall and fight with hope about their problems, while the rest of the people could easily get discouraged and lose hope without finding the purpose to carry on when they hit rock bottom.

The Bible says that the rains and the winds came on both houses: the one built on the rock and the one built on the sand (Matthew 7:24-27). The one on the rock stood firm while the other one was destroyed. This happens in our lives when we don't trust in Jesus. The problems always arrive. The question is how we face them.

That's why a believer could also fail and fall into sin, *but he knows how to rise, and he finds a reason to do it, fight, and resist it*. With this, I don't want to justify or take lightly when someone sins; I am just stating the fact of the benefit of believing in Christ.

After the *crisis/decision stage*, which is the most critical and lasts up to three months, comes the next stage called the *shock stage. It is a period that takes from 1 to 8 months*. During this time, the individuals can even feel physical symptoms of withdrawal, such as confusion, numbness, and inability to concentrate. There might be feelings of desperation and hopelessness.

These statistics are provided by doctors who describe the physical and mental status of most addicts in their time of recovery. What believers might have as an advantage is that having Jesus will help them significantly against feelings of desperation. The withdrawal effect comes to all persons, though. The matter is how we deal with them. Without pornography or any other kind of addiction, we will feel a huge emptiness in us, especially at the very beginning.

We know that Jesus is the one that can fill that void. That's why I am saying that it is an advantage to have Him while we fight with this and any other kind of addiction. Also, people who have never dealt with any kind of addiction need Him as everyone has a void to fill in Himself.

The next stage is called the *grief stage*. It lasts six months. It is the period of time when a person deals with the pain caused by their addiction and supposedly begins to dig into the underlying cause of their porn usage, which can result in deep grieving and emotional turmoil. This happens if we deal properly with our addiction, and it is a necessary part of our way to recovery.

After this comes the *repair stage (18–36 months)*. This is when the person starts focusing on learning balance, self-care, and positive habits that can replace porn. I personally think that this attitude should be present in us since the beginning of recovery. In the beginning, though, as we already said, the person is found in the shock stage, and more effort is required to do that in a proper way.

And at last comes the *growth stage (2+ years)*. This is the final stage, and it is when patients have already a mature outlook on life and their previous relationship with porn. They can look back at their addiction to porn and acknowledge what they have learned. This is when the relationship with partners, family, friends, and kids gets restored and goes through a period of renewal. A person begins to feel appreciation for life and be satisfied. Things get back to normal. We mustn't forget that we always need to be aware and have our shield on.

All these stages and the times they take represent how some specialists in the area have seen this issue through the studies they have undertaken. Timelines and outcomes might differ for different individuals depending on their efforts. We also need to know that regardless of the effort that all of us should place, we need to consider that we are all different; the way the Lord works in us might differ from each other, and our weaknesses might be different.

Nevertheless, we need to put in maximum effort. This is where it comes to our love for the Lord. This is a very important part because it is something required of us. It is important because then the Lord will make things work out for our good—even trials, hard times, and negative experiences.

> "And we know that all things work
> together for good *to those who love
> God*, to those who are the called
> according to *His* purpose." (Romans
> 8:28, emphasis added)

It is very important to love God. Even when we fail, we should ask ourselves, "Did I put in the maximum effort? Did I love God and give it all?" Of course, this doesn't justify the fact that we sinned, but it is different when we give up completely, and we don't fight sin at all.

We need to love God because He loved us. The key to doing it and understanding it is when we experience His love and have it in our hearts. We need to love Him. This will help us a lot in the recovery process. If we missed putting in our best effort and didn't love Him, and for this reason, we failed, then we need to do it at least after that, when we repent and recover.

If we are sincere, we want to recover, we don't want to displease God, and we have faith, He will forgive us after we failed. This is a very important part, and it is a foundation. Still, time is needed for us to rise, heal spiritually, and recover. Samson's hair didn't grow back straight away after he failed. He was surely displeased, but time was needed for him to recover, for his hair to grow, and for him to accomplish God's plan.

Time is needed for us as well, and I hope we don't end up like Samson, losing everything so that we can realize the wrong we were in. Still, we must always have hope and seek to please God. As we already mentioned before in one of the previous chapters, the fear of the Lord is health to our flesh and strength to our bones (Proverbs 3:7–8).

That means that the opposite—the lack of fear of the Lord, which leads to sin—is like a disease for us. Christians get spiritually sick when they sin, and as happens in each disease we experience physically, the same happens spiritually. We lose strength, we are tired, and we even lose appetite, which could be compared to our desire and passion for God.

Time is needed until we regain our full strength. When saying that time is needed, I don't mean a time to be forgiven. *This is the first thing we need to start with after we fail. It should be our foundation, and we can receive it almost immediately when we repent. As believers, we cannot begin recovering without it.*

The Danger of Becoming Lukewarm

Meditating on all of this and on the issues we discuss in this book, there is a passage from the book of Proverbs that comes to my mind:

> "He who loves pleasure *will be* a poor
> man;
> He who loves wine and oil will not be
> rich." (Proverbs 21:17)

This passage is the one that touched my heart in my initial time as a believer. I was new in the faith and just started to know God through the Scriptures. This verse was one of the first that made an impact on my life at that time, and thinking about it, I realize that it is something that is valid throughout our path as Christians.

God probably spoke to me at that time through this verse to place a foundation in my life about how I should live as a believer. Unfortunately, there were times in my life when I didn't pay attention to this teaching, and I ended up in a bad situation. I am not saying that a believer mustn't at all have any pleasures; I am just stating, as this verse says, that he mustn't love them.

We all can have pleasures (I am obviously not speaking about anything sinful here), but we mustn't be driven by them. Instead, we need to be driven by God's guidance and grace, and He will provide for us what we need and let us have pleasure as well, but in the right manner.

Loving pleasures, even though not sinful things, and having them as our main purpose and goal might lead us to do what is sinful, too. We will lose discipline, and in this way, we will neglect looking for the things of God. We must also know that whoever is a newborn believer will have God as his delight. This desire and fire should always be burning in us. There will be times, though, that we will not feel the same, but we need to carry on. Sometimes, there will be trials, and we may not feel so close to God, but this might be a way for us to grow and get to another level in our relationship with God.

Still, when we see that our fire for God gets quenched, we need to take measures. And, at last, loving pleasures could obviously be applied also for the addictions. For any kind of addiction. Addiction steals our time and energy. It is like a parasite. In this way, we don't have and don't find time to seek God and His presence anymore. The priority we had for Him slowly fades away, and we also know that when black and white mix together, they turn into grey.

In this way, we become poor in God. This is what one of the churches in the book of Revelation was warned about (Revelation 3:14–21). Jesus told the church that it needed repentance because it had become lukewarm:

> **14** "And to the angel of the church of the Laodiceans write,
>
> 'These things says the Amen, the Faithful and True Witness, the Beginning of the creation of God: **15** "I know your works, that you are neither cold nor hot. I could wish you were cold or hot. **16** *So then, because you are lukewarm, and neither cold nor hot, I will vomit you out of My mouth.* **17** *Because you say, 'I am rich, have become wealthy, and have need of nothing'—and do not know that you are wretched, miserable, poor, blind, and naked—* **18** I counsel you to buy from Me gold refined in the fire, that you may be rich; and white garments, that you may be clothed, *that* the shame of your nakedness may not be revealed; and anoint your eyes with eye salve, that you may see. **19** As many as I love, I rebuke and chasten. *Therefore*

be zealous and repent. (Revelation 3:14–19, emphasis added)

What was worse was that the church considered itself to be rich when the truth was that it was poor. We need to acknowledge our poverty in front of God. The worst part wasn't that the church was poor but that it couldn't acknowledge its need (poverty). This is what keeps us from getting close to God and becoming really rich in Him. I am obviously talking about being spiritually rich.

What marks our failure in front of God is not the fact that we sinned but that we failed to acknowledge our sins and needs and see that we strayed away from Him. This is what makes us really to be a failure in front of Him. When we, instead, even though falling, still keep on having the desire to be close to God and seek Him, we please Him more.

I am not justifying the fact that we sinned with this. I am saying rather that this is the way to grow and overcome sin. Sometimes, loving pleasure and not acknowledging our need and dependence on God can take us slowly to be far from Him and become lukewarm. This could happen even before we start sinning seriously.

Becoming lukewarm is what displeases God more. This is when we are not sensitive to His voice. Two people could sin. One is a believer who acknowledges his need and poverty in front of God, and the other is a lukewarm person. We can say that the first case is in a better position. The one who is lukewarm should first repent from his attitude and then will be able to acknowledge and fight all the rest of the sins and issues he might be having.

Many times, the major wrong is not only in the sin itself but in the attitude. Remember the story of the Pharisee and the tax collector (Luke 18:9–14)? The one was thankful to God that he was not like others and didn't acknowledge his own sin, while the other wouldn't dare to look up to heaven because he was feeling unworthy and was crying for mercy. Both of them were sinners, but only one was acknowledging it. With the right attitude, we can fight sin in a better way. We cannot produce this attitude with our own strength or capability, and we need to ask God to help us with that.

So, we see that lukewarm people are those who don't acknowledge their need and sin in front of God or even estimate and believe themselves to be good persons or believers who are right with God. They tend to think that they are spiritually rich in front of God.

As we repeatedly said throughout this book, one of the main weapons to fight addiction is to acknowledge our need and that we are in the wrong. So, if we want to fight addiction, we mustn't be at all lukewarm persons.

We need to reject any attempt our heart and mind are trying to push us, telling us that we are not so wrong, and any attempt to justify what we have done. We cannot even justify ourselves by saying that we are victims of various circumstances or the society in which we live. Even if this might be true in part, it is not the right path leading to a solution.

Of course, we mustn't also beat ourselves up and become desperate because our failure and whatever happened is a fact. Time cannot be reversed. We only need to learn from our mistakes, repent, and look forward. Sometimes, a failure in life can make us even stronger than before. This is if we trust in God and follow the right path.

We see the different attitudes held by the Pharisee and the Tax Collector. One thought he was better than others and lived as if everything was fine, while the other acknowledged his wrongs. Our attitude and life should reflect what we truly are—the way we are on the inside—not the other way around.

Because if we attempt to do that by just changing certain outward habits and appearances, we will not succeed. The way we live, behave, and do things cannot change what is inside us. Only God can do that. The people who refuse to change their hearts and hide what is on the inside do that because they don't have faith that it can change. Or perhaps they don't know that what needs to be mainly changed is their heart, and they don't want to do it.

Perhaps they are not aware that religion is not only about following certain customs and traditions or being at peace, but its main purpose is to change lives. That's why the Bible talks of being born again (John 3:1–8). This is a key moment for each person who approaches God, and it needs to happen so that he can become a believer and start his journey with Jesus.

This is the moment when someone repents. Besides experiencing the peace and the blessings of God, a person experiences a radical change in his heart. God doesn't want to deprive you of all the things you like. Yes, some things that are sinful will be taken away, but He will not take all the things you like away from you.

He will let you have them but in the right way. He wants us to live a fulfilled life—a life full of His presence and a life in which you will learn how to enjoy in the best way what He will provide for you.

Notes

[1] "What Does Porn Do to Your Brain? 3 Effects of Porn on the Mind" *Canopy*, 19 Oct. 2020, canopy.us/2020/10/19/what-viewing-pornography-does-to-your-brain. Accessed 10 July 2024.

[2] Doidge, Norman. "Brain Scans of Porn Addicts: What's Wrong With This Picture?" *The Guardian*, 26 Sep. 2013, www.theguardian.com/commentisfree/2013/sep/26/brain-scans-porn-addicts-sexual-tastes. Accessed 10 July 2024.

[3] Cristol, Hope, et al. "Dopamine: What It Is & What It Does" *WebMD*, 09 July 2024, https://www.webmd.com/mental-health/what-is-dopamine. Accessed 28 July 2024.

Leave a review

If you enjoyed this book or found it useful, you are welcome to leave a review on Amazon.com or the store where you purchased it. This will support me and help the book reach other people. I'll also be glad to hear your opinion on the topic.